The Doomsday Survival* Handbook

A Bucket List for Every Conceivable Apocalypse

*Survival not guaranteed

David P. Murphy

Published by Sourcebooks, Inc.
P.O. Box 4410, Naperville, Illinois 60567-4410
(630) 961-3900
Fax: (630) 961-2168
www.sourcebooks.com

Library of Congress Cataloging-in-Publication Data

Murphy, David P.
  The doomsday survivor's handbook : bucket lists for every conceivable apocalypse / David P. Murphy.
    p. cm.
  (pbk. : alk. paper) 1. Survival--Humor. I. Title.
  PN6231.S886M87 2012
  818'.602--dc23
                              2012022254

Printed and bound in the United States of America.
VP 10 9 8 7 6 5 4 3 2 1

Contents

*There will be great earthquakes, famines, and pestilences in various places,
and fearful events and great signs from heaven.*

—*The Holy Bible*

If the apocalypse comes, beep me.

— *Buffy the Vampire Slayer*

Acknowledgments

To my friends and family for your continued belief. And to the folks who read and enjoy these whatever-they-ares—a sincere thank you. But you *do* concern me.

To those folks who helped me to see the absurd light: Woody Allen, the Marx Brothers, Mason Williams, Albert Brooks, Doug Kenney, P. J. O'Rourke, Joel Hodgson, George Carlin, and Bill Cosby.

To my pals Henry and Bob who've lived in interesting times and have braved them with remarkable grace.

A big thanks to David Keif for inspiration with the bass solo bit.

To Cynthia Martin for *really* delivering on the Reapress!

To Peter Lynch—much gratitude.

And, of course, to Laurie Fox for her kindness, talent, and support. And to Gary and Linda at the Agency.

This book has been made possible by the incessant fear mongering of the modern media and that same special quality in our species. You GO, human race!

Introduction

The first question regarding lists like these is usually: "Why?" That's reasonable enough.

Simply put, many of us believe we're invincible and/or ageless, that we're immune to life's inevitable decline. Then, one day, something shifts and we find ourselves fawning over a handgun or paying closer attention to Rogaine ads. That's when it sinks in—we experience our mortality for the first time.

I'm here to tell you there *will* be an ending and most likely it won't come in a pleasant package. Unlike most people, I don't believe existence is going to "vamp till cue." I *know* the end will arrive at my door at 2:00 a.m. like a needy relative looking to "crash on my couch." One sparkling morning, the planet will awaken to horrific news. The multiple news reports will be dire and offer up a spectacle that's pure Independence Day, but with nowhere near its budget for proper effects. And sadly, without Vivica Fox.

It Was the Worst of Times and Then It Got Worserer.

You don't need me to tell you that we live in fearful times. There's not a day goes by that I'm not huddled in a corner of my basement for a short spell because of something I *thought* I heard on the news. It's more than this writer can take, and the crap, in fact, has been scared out of me. Between the giant asteroid, killer flu, chemtrails, and the upcoming robot invasion, the world's taken a running jump onto the Slip-n-Slide of madness. As a result, the hammer's comin' down.

Looking Up the Future's Skirt.

When I do get freaked out, one of the ways I comfort myself is I attempt to see what tomorrow will bring and figure out how best to counteract or cope with such circumstances. No doubt this has to do with my continued fascination with my childhood hero, Nostradamus. Now *there* was a guy who set the bar for peeking into the future, even when his pre-teen skills were limited to accurately predicting what the school cafeteria was serving for lunch the next day. (Note: I possess a complete set of vintage Nostradamus trading cards in mint condition. Eat your hearts out, fanboys!)

When I was a young buck poring over Nostradamus's work, I remember thinking, "What if we could take each potential apocalypse and provide suggestions to help the victims and/or survivors?" In certain cases, the ideas would be about how to best ride out the disaster and, in rare circumstances, how to go out in a blaze of glory. I'm proud to say this is precisely what we've done with this book.

In case you hadn't noticed by now, the concept behind *these* lists differs dramatically from your standard bucket list fare. Here, you'll see none of those humdrum "climb Mount Everest" or "find a way to meet Nancy Grace" sorts of goals. No, *these* are about ensuring your *continued existence*. Achieving your ambitions will *never* happen if you're dead. Right? First things first.

We believe these lists will help you maintain your focus during the unavoidable global chaos. With these at hand, you'll find comfort *and* be able to keep your composure while others lose their shit.

Our? We? Have You Got a Tapeworm or What?

I say "we" because these lists are not mine alone. I'm lucky to have staffers who assisted me in assembling The Lists. We spent valuable time on this—while waiting on hold to bitch at the cable company because that $3.59 credit still hasn't shown up on the latest statement or while XBox Live was off-line yet *again*.

We think we've covered most every probable day of reckoning. We've even included a few of the lesser and/or more obscure Judgment Days, such as a lethal Hasselhoff jingle, the appearance of Galactus, and the dreaded man-eating ponies. No situation was spared, except *The* Situation, who's star is fading and did not make the cut.

I wish I would have had Lists such as these when I went through the Northridge Quake of

1994. Perhaps I would've been better able to endure the humiliation of my apartment building being red-tagged, leaving me incapable of facing my socialite friends for weeks. Instead, I spent the first few days hyperventilating under the futon with four cats, attempting to elude the imagined gangs of looters.

By the Way, What's with the Format of These Lists? And Who's the Hot Skeleton Chick?

Please stop skipping around the book.

The Lists are broken up into five parts: The Sacred, The Cosmic, The Invasions, The Man-Made, and The Naturally Occurring. With each disaster, you'll find a handy synopsis of how it will unfold, how long it will last, the percentage of the populace affected, and a List of suggestions instructing the reader how to deal with said disaster. (Let's face it—there's not much to be done in some of these cases—hence, fewer nuggets of advice.)

We're also proud to introduce our spokesmodel for The Lists, The Grim Reapress. That's correct, the Specter of Death gave itself a major makeover and is now sporting a steamy new look (and wardrobe) that better suits our current society. The Reapress will rate each doomsday—from zero to ten, ten being the best for her and the worst for us—and offer up her unique perspective. Welcome aboard, G. R.!

I Can Take Whatever Life Throws at Me.

Admittedly, these lists may not be for everyone. Perhaps you're one of those hardcore individuals who will throw him- or herself into the apocalyptic fray in a fearless Will Smith–like manner. Bully for you. Most of us at The Lists (the team that's helping to bring you this book) aren't like you and we believe most people are like us—happy to have instructions to follow in an emergency. We don't want to be improvising our way up the I-5, trying to get to our corporate panic vault before the Planet Eater arrives.

Personally, I'm *not* a guy who's capable of going into the woods naked and coming out three days later in a fabulous hand-sewn beaver suit. Nor would I be smoking a cigar rolled from wild tobacco and carrying a satchel full of freshly carved venison steaks. In other words, I need all the help I can get.

And I bet you do too, or you wouldn't still be reading this disaster of an intro.

All Right, We Get the Idea—You're a Wuss.

Here's my take: Keep your eyes on the skies, follow the news as needed, and when the Shinola truly hits the fan, hang on to this book. By having it at the ready and cross-referencing whichever manner of awful arrives, you'll have a honey do list that'll keep you calm. That along with the Xanax.

On behalf of myself and everyone at The Lists, happy endings to all and to all a good night. Skeeter bless!

David P. Murphy
Frazier Park Panic Vault
Hunkered down in the twenty-first century

Part 1

The Sacred:
Putting the "Die" in "Deity"

The Rapture!

The Grim Rating

Meh—6.5

"A tad disappointing, but I might use the floaters for target practice!"

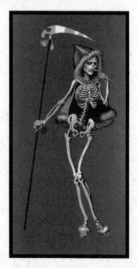

How It'll Go Down: The Rapture feels like an autumnal event, not unlike Homecoming—or Oktoberfest, but with limited beer selections. As we understand it, right before the Rapture begins, a tall guy riding a chariot will appear in the sky. And how does *that* work? Is he in everyone's sky everywhere, and, if so, what kinda pricey gear is behind *that*? Anyway, this fella pulls up in his chariot (which many believe is made of dark chocolate), gives the planet the hairy eyeball, pulls out a krumhorn, and takes a solo, which goes on three choruses too long. (You don't hear much solo krumhorn and, after *he* solos, you'll know why.)

   Then, if you've been nice and not naughty, you'll get to float away with him and other God-fearing folk. Yup, float. Without any prompting or lessons of any kind, you'll suddenly be flying, all the while staring down at the non-floaters (or "statics") left behind, yelling something mean like "Told ya so!"

Estimated Length of Disaster: Three to four hours, but expect problems in larger urban areas where floaters could experience gridlock and delays. Additionally, a few of the more aggressive statics will be attempting to hold on to floaters in order to tag along. That'll slow everything down. Remember: Floaters are souls that are about to be saved—they're not hot air balloons. Get an afterlife.

Percentage of Population Affected: Everyone, or to use a number often referenced by *Maury* show guests, 1000%.

Whether you end up as a floater or a static, here's your list:

RAPTURE BUCKET LIST

☐ Change into clean, modest underwear in case you're "chosen." You don't want the entire world peeking up your dress and seeing a thong. Or a skid mark.

☐ Score a lot of Dramamine. Floating in the air for any length of time can lead to motion sickness. And we hear there may be long waits on the Eternal Tarmac. Worst part: while on the Tarmac, they don't serve snacks.

☐ Be in touch with your family. You might not be seeing them again anytime soon. Especially that cousin who dated outside of your faith.

☐ If you're not chosen, try not to pout. Throwing a Hades-themed party might cheer you up. Purchase devilishly clever party favors, make flaming appetizers and blood-colored punch. After the last guest leaves, barricade your home—it's gonna get messy out there!

☐ Stay hopeful; work on your fear of heights.

☐ If you see Larry Flynt, run.

☐ Rumor has it that the chariot guy loves it when folks "jam" with him, and if he sees you playing along while he's doing his krumhorn shtick, he might have a change of heart concerning your awful fate. (Does Guitar Center stock krumhorns?)

☐ Have additional warmer-climate clothing on hand in case you end up being a static. A crapload of Tylenol also wouldn't hurt.

☐ While floating, it's considered bad form to shout across the distance between you and your fellow floaters. A brief nod of acknowledgment is acceptable along with the royal wave.

S'tan!

The Grim Rating:

S'tan's the Man! 10.0!!

"Right now-ow-ow I consider myself-elf-elf the luckiest Specter of Death-eath-eath on the face-ace-ace of the Earth. Whan S'tan calls, I'm sooo there. Like shootin' souls in a barrel!"

How It'll Go Down: Whaddya know—it turns out Halloween really *is* Satan's day.

On October 31, 2027, Satan (or "S'tan" as he prefers) will make himself known to the world in a showy fashion. He'll take over the airwaves, which even a staunch Christian has to admit is kind of impressive.

S'tan will inform us that he and God have worked out a deal whereby S'tan gets Earth as part of a cosmic trade. God is apparently hot for Mars and Europa, the latter having been recommended after a lengthy chat with the Monoliths. (Sometimes you *can't* get those Monoliths to shut up.) S'tan was a sport and not only gave up the planet/moon combo, but also threw in the Kuiper Belt, a gently used pair of Birkenstocks in God's size, and a third-round draft pick in 2029.

This deal doesn't bode well for Earth. Since we'll no longer be under God's divine protection, S'tan will make our planet his bitch. We'll become his playground, his laboratory, and his performance venue of choice. And from everything we hear, that dude has an *awesome* imagination.

Estimated Length of Disaster: It'll take a day or so for everyone on the planet to understand the full implications of S'tan's plans and then all hell will break loose. Literally.

Percentage of Population Affected: No one is overlooked. He's nothing if not thorough.

Here's your damned list:

S'TAN BUCKET LIST

☐ Start admiring the artwork of Hieronymus Bosch. He was *way* closer than anyone ever thought.

☐ Get used to the idea that you could end up with horns and/or striking red skin. Check your wardrobe to see which outfits will complement that hue.

☐ No secret bunkers or hideaways are going to help you. S'tan's got Santa Claus beat hands down in the omniscience department.

☐ When the Dark Collector comes to visit, you'd be advised to leave your soul in a bag by the door—and a rooster if you've got one.

☐ Remember: S'tan takes many forms. He may appear to you as a snake salesman, a large red spider in your tub, or even a smokin' hostess at a nearby diner. Beware of anything unusual and anyone other than your closest friends and family. For that matter, keep an eye on them too.

- If you don't bag up your soul, you could get into a battle with The Grinder, one of the Dark Collector's creepier henchmen. Know this: One way to fend off The Grinder is to clear your mind of all images other than puppies and rainbows. The Grinder can't endure such sweetness and it may cause him to ralph.

- S'tan's a sucker for flattery. Butter him up and maybe he'll make it quick. Trust us: you'll want any fate other than eternal damnation. That's too exhausting.

- After S'tan redecorates the globe in a Bosch-inspired manner, Las Vegas will change little.

- Friends and family members who've always been extremely religious will be particularly bummed. Comfort them as much as possible. (Except for the ones who were *so* judgmental and called you a heathen. Screw them.)

- Unfriend Mia Farrow on Facebook.

Holy Wars!

The Grim Rating:

A total letdown—3.4

"I had such high hopes for this one. Seemed like a match made in heaven, as it were. Such psychotic passion usually produces better results. Oh well, they'll end up squaring off again—they always do."

How It'll Go Down: Everything old and stupid becomes new and stupid again with a timeless battle royale! In this corner, we've got the Christians, feeling positive about their popularity over the last few centuries. And in this corner, we've got the Muslims, a religion on the rise and not about to take flack from anyone. It was only a matter of time before these two titans squared off once more, and what better location than northern Africa?

Yes, it's "Visa® presents The New, Improved Crusades™" and this

rematch is going to be *big*. Not only Catholics versus the Muslims, but this time around, the Catholics will be joined by a bunch of Protestants, and in a completely unexpected development, lots of Mormons too! Who saw that comin'? It will be an alignment for the ages, almost like the Super Friends.

It begins innocently enough. In the foothills of the Atlas Mountains of Tunisia, construction crews will be working on the ill-conceived CarthageLand theme park. One morning, an elderly foreman will be summoned to determine what's halted progress on the Monorail of Shame. He'll find his workers gathered around what appears to be a recently unearthed archaic picnic basket. Without thinking, he'll kneel next to the basket and open the lid. A searing white light will burst forth, and the sounds of a soprano-heavy choir will be heard as the foreman reaches into the basket to find a glistening chalice. As he picks it up, his body glows and his gray hair turns jet black. In awe, the workers fall to the ground, bow to the chalice, and take photos with their phones.

Once these pics hit the Internet, the chess pieces move briskly. The Vatican will ask to see the chalice, be denied, and then sulk. The owners of CarthageLand will say the chalice is theirs and it will become part of an exhibit at the park. An interfaith council of theologians, scientists, and Photoshop experts will study the chalice pics and declare that it is, indeed, the Holy Grail. When the Vatican and the council press the point with the owners again, words will be exchanged and hurtful things said that can't be taken back. Much of the planet will think, "Here we go again."

Estimated Length of Disaster: It will go on and on and on—same as it ever was.

Percentage of Population Affected: Fewer than you'd think. Surprisingly, only about 52% of the population will care about the classic conflict. The rest would prefer that folks simply try to get along with one another. Apparently, that's too much to ask.

Behold—the shining list!

HOLY WARS BUCKET LIST

☐ Beware the Bahaï'is—they'll push to be included in the struggle as "refs." Their interpretation of the rules of combat could heavily influence the final outcome. We say let the players play and don't make any ticky-tack calls.

☐ Atheists and agnostics—it's good to be you! Chances are you can ride this one out.

☐ Extremists on both sides can be blowy-uppy. Keep your guard up around those with bulky vests or oversized hoodies.

☐ North Africa sure is balmy. Make sure you stay hydrated during the conflicts. The latest conflict-inspired sports drink, Crus-Ade, is supposedly a fine product and there was no fee involved with this mention. None.

☐ Remember: Your idea of a "Crescent Cross" will probably not help develop a compromise between the two sides. Those folks are workin' through a lot ancient shit, man. Nice try, though.

☐ See if anyone can get their God on the horn and find out who He's rooting for. One would hope He's staying neutral. We know Skeeter is.

☐ Complain to Amnesty International about the Christians using pork bombs. While the concept sounds delicious, such a device is highly unethical and goes directly against Article 3.2.a of the Hooved-Meat Provisions of the Geneva Convention.

☐ Splurge for the pay-per-view twenty-four-hour service in month nine. Things will start to *really* rock right about then.

☐ Try pitching a Simon Cowell–produced *Ululation Idol* to help bring people together.

Plague of Locusts!

The Grim Rating:

Less than the author thinks—6.3

"So it's come down to bugs helping me out. Sometimes I think I'm gonna hurl because of these scenarios. And I'm supposed to be okay with this? What's next: a holy entity named Skeeter? Oh shit, that *is* what's next. Damn me!"

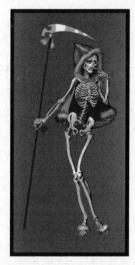

How It'll Go Down: This one could qualify for a spot in any of three different categories, but it feels so Biblical to us, we just *had* to put it here.

As harvest season begins in 2031, the morning sun peeks through the ammonia vapors as the worker-bots don their best overalls to man the auto-threshers. Suddenly, dark clouds appear. These will not be ordinary clouds or even part of one of the megastorms that now form regularly and make celebrity meteorologists faint. No, these clouds will be composed of jillions of hungry bugs coming for all things edible.

Genetic modification of our food will have caused a serious problem. (Hey, we're simply reporting the future facts.) Everyday locusts will respond to the modified grain like ball players to steroids, bulking up quicker than you can say "Barry Bonds." This will lead to a transmuted specie of super locust—one capable of eating more, reproducing more, and flying farther. This locust will prefer a well-rounded meal and will decide that the life of an herbivore is too bland. That's when it'll start dabbling in any form of available flesh. Along with plants, animal life *and* humans will also be attacked by the winged demons. Even packaged foods will fear for their well-being—nothing will be safe from the bugs. The lone exception: Velveeta.

Estimated Length of Disaster: It'll be three years before the planet's resources are exhausted and the locusts turn to eating each other.

Percentage of Population Affected: About 90%. The colder regions will have a leg up on the rest of us, but you arctic dwellers better hope the locusts don't adapt or figure out how to make small furry overcoats.

Chew on this:

PLAGUE OF LOCUSTS
BUCKET LIST

☐ Along with Velveeta, Brut Cologne is something the bugs find to be repugnant. (Re-bug-nant?) Consequently, hose down yourself and your family with the fetid fluid.

☐ If you happen to be grocery shopping when the insects arrive, huddle close to the Velveeta display. Fit your body into the cooler (if it's stored there). You'll be safer.

☐ Setting fire to your crops will do almost no good. Sure, you might kill a few hundred thousand bugs, but that's a drop in the bucket. We don't mean to be a drag, but unless everyone burns their crops, it's not going to matter. If you want to organize a festive Crop-Burning Day event through social media sites, knock yourself out. Where's that "'invite planet" check box?

☐ Encourage the military to throw the Prairie states under the bus—that'll buy the rest of us some time.

☐ Reprogram the robot farmers to be your first line of defense. Dress 'em up as much as possible to make the idiot insects think they're humans. That way, when the bugs bite down, they'll be all, like, "clank" and "ow."

☐ If you own livestock, invite them into your home. Get bunk beds for the chickens and futons for the pigs. The cows will be fine with a throw rug. (Nightshirts?)

☐ Make a sign that points to your neighbor's house that reads "Good eats here!"

☐ Project idea: Create a custom jumpsuit made of carbon-fiber insect netting. A tad revealing perhaps, but it will be worth every bit of the time and expense.

Skeeter Snaps His Fingers and Keels Us!

The Grim Rating:

Not too shabby—8.1.

"Okay, so this Skeeter might not be bad after all. Call me old-fashioned, but I dig a short fuse in a god. Let the wrath begin, baby!"

How It'll Go Down: Many of us here at The Lists share a common belief in a Universal Creator known to us as "Skeeter." Skeeter is probably very similar to your God, but our Skeeter is infinitely more powerful. Does *your* God have heat vision? We didn't think so.

As a result of our dedication to this divine spirit, we're more peaceful individuals. Sure, one or two of us have had meltdowns since we "found" Skeeter, but said meltdowns usually involved the 405 Freeway in Southern California. What can we say—we've all got triggers.

As far as how we feel about Skeeter, we keep our beliefs to ourselves and try not to proselytize, although I'll admit I show off my wallet-sized photo of Him to anyone who'll let me. We commune with Him frequently and, if our prayers go straight to voicemail, we don't take it personally. We know in our hearts that He's probably on a tech support call and will get back to us as soon as He's able. We're not looking for approval from others and we don't care whether or not people understand that, at 5 p.m. every Tuesday, our faith requires us to wear dickeys and adorn a goat with garlands.

We could talk about Skeeter all day, but let's get back to the disaster.

Facts are facts: The human race has made a mess of the planet. We're not nice to the flora or fauna, nor are we kind to each other. Skeeter will finally get wind of this and it won't sit well with Him. (Benevolent He may be, but His fuse is considered diminutive.) This is why, one day, not long from now, He'll hit the wall and begin thinning the human herd. With no warning whatsoever, people will keel over as if they've been unplugged. Skeeter will use His Lord And Master Database to determine who deserves to live and who—well, you know. This form of downsizing will cause anxiety for folks who are observing the keeling while waiting for the other shoe salesman to drop. Therapists, this windfall is yours!

Estimated Length of Disaster: The scariest part will be how quickly this will happen—all within a couple of days, proving that our Skeeter is every bit as efficient as He is loving!

Percentage of Population Affected: The Lord And Master Database will indicate that only about 17.8% of the population deserves to live. (That Database is sooooo Old Testament.) The aftermath of this event will create a chaotic era where those remaining will need to learn new skills in a hurry—like how the hell to keep utilities running.

Skeeter wants you to love this:

SKEETER'S WRATH BUCKET LIST

☐ Start volunteering at homeless shelters, tithing in excess, adopting kids, sponsoring elephant sanctuaries, and anything else you can do to counteract the spiritual stains that still linger from your four years in that fraternity.

☐ If you're simply evil and incapable of change, then have a bang-up time while you can, but get your affairs in order.. You're getting unplugged soon.

☐ Study the work of Mother Teresa. You don't have to go full-bore leper lover, but you could sure stand to have some of her humility and grace rub off on you. And by the way, making a big deal out of your altruistic acts will negate whatever progress you're making. Mmmkay?

☐ Hand out candy to kids every day of the year. And dollar bills.

☐ If you're the type of individual who has *people*, give them generous severance packages and send them on their way. Would it kill you to lead your own life and reflect on it every now and then?

☐ If you work for any of the top five international banks, there's no need to read any further. Verily, your soul has been foreclosed upon and your *eviction* is coming.

☐ Statistically speaking, certain job categories have better survival rates than others. Teachers have a relatively high likelihood of remaining alive, while corporate bankruptcy lawyers and oil company lobbyists tilt the needle in the opposite direction. Figure out where you fall between those two and you'll have an accurate picture of your future.

☐ Skeeter has something special planned for rhino poachers. Your bones will be ground to dust while you're still alive. That's gonna sting!

☐ No kittens shall be keeled.

☐ Do your best to stay focused on a higher plane. You really don't want your final thought to be "Hey, get a load of the bazooms on that chi—".

Ghosts and Demons!

The Grim Rating:

WTF?! A crummy 3.1.

"Ghosts are lame and demons aren't far behind. Get over yourselves—you're dead. Quit subjecting everyone to your angst and sorrow—you're encroaching on *my* gig!"

How It'll Go Down: We thought this might be an invasion, but Skeeter told us this entry belonged in the Sacred category. Skeeter knows best.

During an upcoming summer solstice celebration at Stonehenge, one of the druid wannabes will mispronounce a mystic phrase. The rock known as the "Heel Stone," which is seated outside the circle of other stones (because it misbehaved in 1842 BC), will then begin to glow. This luminescence will become brighter until finally a beam of green light shoots out of the Heel Stone, zapping the earthy center of the monument.

Unfortunately, this will open a door between our plane of existence and the etheric plane, which, as we all know, is lousy with demons and phantoms. What follows will be a mass migration of goblins and ghosts into our realm, making it an Ellis Island for the deceased.

During this invasion, our globe will be besieged by spirits in a sporadic manner. In other words, certain areas get it worse than others. The United Kingdom and its creaky olde energy will take it in the shorts, along with most of Europe. Wyoming? Fairly quiet.

One upside: about half the ghosts and demons will be thrilled to be free from their former dimension and, therefore, disinterested in scaring people. According to the grapevine, there are massive shortcomings in the etheric plane—chronic plumbing issues and poor access to good knishes. To these interlopers, our dimension, by comparison, will seem like paradise. Go figure.

Estimated Length of Disaster: Unless someone discovers a way to close that door at Stonehenge, this scenario will be ongoing.

Percentage of Population Affected: 27–38%. Sure there'll be damage, but this isn't a complete groovekill (except for you Europeans—you'll undoubtedly feel the pinch).

Boo! Here's the list:

GHOSTS AND DEMONS BUCKET LIST

☐ Put together a supernatural team made up of David Blaine, Lance Burton, Criss Angel, and The Amazing Jonathan. Penn and Teller can come along too if they start to whine. The team's super assignment: close the portal by whatever means necessary. Then tell us what number we're thinking of.

☐ Break out the Ouija Board. That thing is gonna be a chatterbox!

☐ If a demon decides to move into your attic or bedroom wall, it might be prudent to ask it if there's anything it needs. A toad? An eyelash from an insurance agent? Chaw?

☐ Acclimate quickly to the idea that life will now be full of horrifying creatures—even worse than a political convention.

☐ Burning sage is considered to be one way to dispel negative juju. Buy a shit ton of sage.

☐ Be on guard for that Stay Puft dude.

☐ Start watching those paranormal programs again. They'll be much more action packed!

☐ Prepare for the eventuality that a few of your dead relatives might drop by. When they do, point out it's a bad time for a visit and ask if you can put them up at the nearby Holiday Inn Express. You hear the complimentary omelet bar is terrif!

☐ Berate a Druid any chance you get. Dumb Druids.

The GodSaw!

The Grim Rating:

Annoying variables—3.8.

"This pisses me off. How am I supposed to accurately score that which can't be accurately scored? And when did I start talking like a Zen master? Hey, SawBoy, just do what you're supposed to do! Is that so *hard*?!"

How It'll Go Down: The legend of a celestial fix-it shoppe is true—a place where He keeps all of His tools on a majestic pegboard as massive as the Glatni Ringbelt. There, every utensil of creation and uncreation is always available for Him so that He may tweak, repair, refurbish, or demolish existence to suit His capricious needs.

And so it will come to be that one day, as He's being distracted by a series of collapsing stars far, far away, He'll exit the shoppe in a hurry, accidentally leaving his circular saw running for a couple of eons.

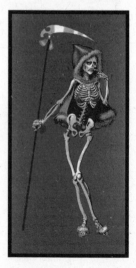

During that time, the so-called GodSaw (by Craftsman) will vibrate off the Almighty Workbench, fall through the heavenly skies, and end up floating freely in our cosmos. Unfortunately, it'll land in the Milky Way and be on a collision course with Earth.

(Note from the staff of The Lists: we would've preferred to call this the "SkeeterSaw" but went with the more conventional "GodSaw" to mollify the readership. You're welcome.)

As you can imagine, the Sacred Saw is dad-gum large, and how it intersects with the planet will determine the extent of the damage done. The good news is that we might make it onto the next season of His show *Flip This Planet* on TRN. (Programming note: The Righteousness Network is currently a part of certain subscription packages and may not be available in your area.)

Estimated Length of Disaster: If the Saw slices the outside edge of our planet and only takes "a little off the top," the disaster will last a few hours. If it instead hits us in the ol' breadbasket, it'll take a couple of days and Earth will be halved. That'll be *no bueno*.

Percentage of Population Affected: Anywhere from 2–100%. Location, location, location.

Cut to the list:

GODSAW BUCKET LIST

☐ Once the trajectory has been established, erect an adamantium shield around the coordinates where the blade will first make contact. That'll screw it up!

☐ Send a manned mission to either sever the incredibly long extension cord or remove the holy battery pack.

☐ Coordinate an effort to have everyone on the planet jump up and down at the exact same moment to see if we can shift our orbit enough to make the Saw miss us.

☐ If, as some speculate, adamantium is fictional (yeah, right!), make the shield out of diamonds instead, which will look like our planetary armor's been bedazzled. Cool!

☐ Throw Mars at the Saw—see if that slows it down.

☐ Organize a prayer chain that will ask God to pick up His stuff.

☐ No calling the Saw a "tool"—best not to hurt its feelings.

☐ Coordinate a planetwide defense effort with Bob Vila. That guy is *always* full of handy ideas. And he sure can rock the plaid!

☐ Ask David Copperfield to make the Earth disappear right before the Saw hits. And then have him bring us right back! Oooooo, magic!

Part 2

The Cosmic: Bang/Whimper/Whatever

A Giant Asteroid!

The Grim Rating:
A perfect 10!!
"Winner, winner, dead chicken dinner!"

How It'll Go Down: One fine morning, the planet will wake up to the words of Bruce Willis being translated into every language and broadcast on global television and radio networks. He'll be informing us of our impending doom. The good-natured Mr. Willis will have been asked to do this to lend more legitimacy to the dire message. Even so, roughly one-third of the planet will not have access to radio or TV or will blow it off, believing this to be an ad for his ill-timed upcoming movie, *Armageddon II: The Meteor's Revenge*. The two-thirds who listen will hear a story about a rogue asteroid the size of Australia that broke out of its orbit when, several months ago, it was rudely bumped by an

enormous space creature named Yorggh. Because of this run-in, the asteroid is now headed toward Earth. When Mr. Willis utters the phrases "forty-eight hours from now" and "extinction event," you'll be able to hear an ear-piercing collective scream anywhere on the globe. Talk about a wall of sound

Estimated Length of Disaster: Oh, it won't take long after that rock plows into us. Two days tops, depending on where you live.

Percentage of Population Affected: Everyone, everything. It's all goin' dark, doc.

Since there's no hope of survival for any living thing, the following list may do little to help, but try to have fun anyway!

GIANT ASTEROID BUCKET LIST

☐ Make a point of telling everyone you truly love how much you love them and *then* start drinking—*don't* do it the other way around. You'd regret spending your final two days telling complete strangers how much they've meant to you.

☐ Buy a telescope. Sure, the end is gonna be bad, but it should be a terrific show and a real popcorn event!

☐ In this case, turn off the news channels— they're bound to be downers.

☐ When looting your nearby grocery store, arrive early, get all the stuff you've been craving, and exit briskly. Don't stop to read food labels—none of that matters now. Cook everything as quickly as possible before the power grid gets shaky, which should occur within hours.

☐ For the luvva Pete, make love as much as you can. Celibates, give it up.

- [ ] When looting your favorite electronics store, treat yourself to the biggest and priciest flat-panel TV you can find. You're going out in style!

- [ ] Explain to the kids that it's all done with CGI. They don't need to know the truth and who needs the crying? There'll be enough of that from the adults.

- [ ] Buy plenty of Preparation H because those things are painful and you're gonna n—oh, that's *asteroid.*

- [ ] During the riots, remember that there are still certain protocols to be followed. For example, the people with Molotov cocktails *always* go to the front of the line. And when jumping on cop cars, you're *required* to flail. It's in *The Rioter's Handbook.*

Space Pirates!

The Grim Rating:

Long on activity, short on action—5.8.

"The Bruntosans wreak absolute havoc with my inventory system and I'm starting to get cheesed. They keep moving species around; I can't keep up and I'm going through secretaries like toilet paper. It might be time to lower the boom on these wankers."

How It'll Go Down: This could be considered an invasion, but it has an intergalactic vibe that simply screams "cosmic."

What a perfectly ghastly scenario! The Bruntosa, an unusually brutal and wily race whose home planet is hidden deep in the Glatni Ringbelt, make a living as space pirates. (Well, not exactly a living, but they get by.) Their MO is to kidnap the population of planets and then sell them to other races who need slaves, or at least creatures to do light housekeeping.

Interesting fact: Instead of parrots on their shoulders, these pirates have large, leech-like creatures attached to the sides of their heads. Each considers the other its pet.

Bruntosan researchers will study Earth and attempt to decipher programs like *The Apprentice* and *Undercover Boss*. They'll come to the conclusion that Earthlings would make excellent underlings and that our planet would be a perfect candidate for a hostile takeover.

And so, in June 2039, dozens of their hypno-ships begin orbiting our planet. These vehicles are referred to as "hypno-ships" because at the bottom of each ship is an enormous swirling disc that resembles the hypno-coins in ancient comic book ads. Anyone who stares into the sky and at the ships will, within about twenty to twenty-five seconds, lose their free will. At that point, the device senses the victim's slave state and signals the ship's transport beams to pull the poor schmuck into the ship's hold. Once there, everyone is fitted with doggie collars, which serve no purpose other than to be degrading and kinky.

Once each ship is packed with slaves, the victims will be taken to an intergalactic auction to be sold to the highest bidders. Another interesting fact: alien auctioneers talk approximately three and a half times faster than their human counterparts and roughly four octaves higher.

Note: This disaster is not to be confused with The Rapture. There *will* be people floating in the air, but they *won't* be going to a better place.

Estimated Length of Disaster: Unfortunately, there'll be a fleet of ships, each with a big-ass hold, and it'll take quite a while to fill 'er up. Also, the Bruntosans have been known to stack victims like cordwood, which makes the process take longer. (Humans don't stack well.) As for the length of time, all told, up to a month.

Percentage of Population Affected: Over 67%.

Don't we need the word "matey" in here somewhere?

SPACE PIRATES BUCKET LIST

☐ Don't stare at the ships! A simple solution really, but a few billion folks won't be able to resist the urge. Lotsa luck with that slave life then.

☐ Women might want to get their Princess-Leia-gold-metal-bikini act together. The more fetching you can be, the better your chance for a lighter workload—that is, unless your new masters find you desirable, which will really blow.

☐ Apologies go out in advance to those in Earth's population who are touchy about the slave concept. Just know that everyone will be in the same boat/ship, as the case may be. This will be an equal-opportunity-for-misery event.

☐ If you're one of those people who knows you're going to end up looking at the ships and fall into the thrall of the pirates, pack lots of jerky and juice boxes in your pants. Get a pair of those cargo pants with umpteen pockets because then there'll be plenty of places to store treats. Bottom line: the food on the ships reportedly sucks—plates of dying larva and a black liquid that the Bruntosans think is like Cristal and it so isn't.

☐ Don't ever touch one of the leeches on the Bruntosans. If you do, the creature will immediately subdivide and attach to you too. You don't look good in hats, especially Gaga-esque meaty ones.

☐ Here's a picture-perfect plan: in advance of the pirates' arrival, have yourself profession-ally hypnotized so that you'll be resistant to the Bruntosan hypno-ships. Suck it, pirates!

☐ Head over to your neighborhood Jimbo's Porn-Pourri Mart and snag a doggie collar. You might as well start getting used to it. It might even become, dare we say, fetching on you.

☐ If you end up on the auction block, try to summon the will to affect the bidding. Twitch or do something dumb. Why? Because there are two bidding species to avoid. One will grind you up for filler in their pet foods and another will require you to give them daily tongue baths. Both gigs are a nightmare. So, if you appear to be dam-aged goods, they'll be less likely to snap you up, matey.

☐ If you actually make it through this disaster and find yourself still on Earth, it's going to be sweet. Move into a mansion, drive a Porsche off a dealership's lot, etc. The sky's the limit!

The Moon Breaks Out of Orbit!

The Grim Rating:

Should've been a 10, ended up a 5.6.

"I don't like to brag, but it was I who convinced the Moon it could do better. I kept texting it that it deserved more than what Earth was offering and that maybe the mighty blue planet needed to find out what it would be like to have no moon. Ain't I a stinkuh?"

How It'll Go Down: Without naming names, certain celestial bodies are weenies and, boy howdy, we've got one living near us. Let's just say its name rhymes with "swoon." Get the drift?

It'll be during one of those harvest moon nights several years from now. Couples will be taking in the lunar splendor and making out in the backseat of their electric cars, which will be a tight fit. That's right when the wussy satellite will decide it's had it with playing second

fiddle to our planet. It'll break out of orbit, claiming it's always wanted to see the asteroid belt in Autumn. The Moon believes it might fit in better with the more similarly proportionate "roids." And *that's* the word the Moon will use—*roids*! What an idiot!

Be that as it may, this moon-walkabout isn't going to pan out so well for Earth. Oceans and lakes are gonna go apeshit and spill all over the place. Surfing will suck. Couples will have no option left but to stare at low-wattage light bulbs. The birthrate will plummet. Romance too will take a body check into the glass. Pfizer will release a new pill—Fervolon—a sort of Viagra equivalent that will claim to "engorge your dormant romantic notions."

Estimated Length of Disaster: Hard to say. It could be a while if the Moon decides it doesn't miss us. Sigh.

Percentage of Population Affected: If you're on the planet (and we're betting you are), you're bound to be affected.

By the light of the silvery list:

ERRANT MOON BUCKET LIST

☐ If you live near water, line your property with industrial rolls of Brawny.

☐ Seek government aid in your plan to launch a number of artificial moons that you've designed to counter the lack of gravitational pull. Sure, these faux moons are on the dinky side, but if you put 4,300 or 4,400 of 'em into orbit, it could make a real difference to Earth. (It might, you don't know: you're not the boss of the planet.)

☐ During the grieving period, when the Earth will miss its moon, the ground may get wobbly. This can cause motion sickness in some and violent death in others. Do your best to stay in the "motion sickness" column.

☐ The Earth's orbit will be negatively impacted and result in a merger of the seasons. In the end, only two will remain: sprall and sumter. They'll both be dreadful. Performances of *Porgy and Bess* will now include the haunting "Sumtertime."

☐ On top of the wobbling, as the planet adjusts to its gravitational realities, it may begin to vibrate. Like, *all* the freakin' time. Women will enjoy this more than men.

☐ If you happen to be that prunish alarmist Harold Camping, listen up: The Moon may take a sabbatical and there *will* be chaos, but it's *still* not the end of the world. *Again*.

☐ Paste a moon stencil on your window of whatever phase was your fondest. Stare wistfully.

☐ Learn from your mistakes. Next time you have a celestial body orbiting you, be nicer to it. Take it out, show it off, and buy it stuff.

☐ Is this a valid excuse to start that snake-collecting hobby you've always wanted to pursue? Probably not, but it's worth asking.

☐ When sprall rolls around, make sure you rake up all the leaves before the firestorms and snows start. Don't leave that chore until sumter—you'll be shoveling wet ash.

Cosmic Orgasm Wave Intersects with Earth!

The Grim Rating:

Better for you than it was for me—1.9.

"Yeah, Earth, you're a real stud. Forty-three seconds in and—kablooey—it's over. What a joke. Even the Specter of Death likes a little foreplay. Don't bother to call, okay? You're dead to me."

How It'll Go Down: Maybe we should rephrase that…

How It Will Occur: Now *this* one we like! A mystic event will occur in the summer of 2018. A neural energy wave will travel across the cosmos and pass through the Earth in mid-July causing simultaneous forty-three-second-long orgasms for every living creature on the planet. Even ferns. While this, at first, may not sound like a disaster, think about it: planes are flying, people are

driving, ferns are ferning, etc. Not the most convenient time to cream your jeans, know what we're sayin'?

Anywho, this startling sensory experience will be more than certain people's tickers can take and lives *will* be lost, although most will die wearing a grin.

Estimated Length of Disaster: One day, but the ramifications will last for weeks.

Percentage of Population Affected: 100% affected, 100% satisfied. (*There's* a new one!) And a couple million dead.

Oh baby, oh baby, take my list:

ORGASM WAVE BUCKET LIST

☐ As the entire planet lights up cigarettes in the afterglow, incredible tobacco clouds form and lead to nicotine rainfall. Enjoy the buzz!

☐ Implore scientists to find a way to bring back the wave. (Offer the wave a promise ring?)

☐ If you're one of the unlucky ones who happen to be driving when it hits (or on a scaffold or something similarly steeped in bad timing), keep your eyes open, breathe deeply, and ride it out.

☐ And for those who will be asleep when the wave hits, don't feel bad about the sheets— it'll come out in the wash.

☐ If you've been frigid or impotent and nothing has helped your condition, you'll find that your nervous system has been rebooted and you may not have such issues anymore. Throw away the gels and pills!

☐ You may experience a conversation similar to this: "You know, Bob, that summary motion you handed me was not at all what I was—oooh–wow–what the—helllllllllllllllloooooo!"

☐ Find out how it was for Meg Ryan.

☐ For those rare few that may have been making love during the event (or squirreled away in a closet doing the unmentionable), this "double dipping" may cause you problems. There could be memory loss and oodles of drool for the first 48 hours to 7 weeks.

☐ Afterward, have pancakes. Right?

☐ Make sure sex addicts understand it wasn't their doing. No reparations or apologies are needed.

That Planet Eater Thing from *Star Trek*!

The Grim Rating:

Ding, Dong, the Earth is Dead—10.0!

"Shatner has eluded my grasp for long enough! Right before the Eater unleashes its deathbeam, Shatner will die, unless, of course, he wants to do me!"

How It'll Go Down: According to star charts and our dear friend who's a major frickin' Trekkie—shout out to Ensign First Class Richie!—the Planet Eater is due to enter Earth's orbit in late 2028. Since Shatner will probably still be alive (after having many parts replaced by bio-organic devices), he'll be allowed first shot at negotiating (because he *was* "The Negotiator") with the only known doomsday device that resembles a mile-long turd.

When the Eater fails to recognize Shatner and asks instead for Spock,

Bill will take it personally and storm out of the room, which, in this case, is a multimedia booth in D.C. That's projecting his image onto the moon. Once the Eater realizes Nimoy's a no-show, the dining extravaganza begins, making Adam Richman look like a total wimp.

Estimated Length of Disaster: This will go *very* south *very* quickly. Once the Eater gets crankin'—and that dude can *hoove!*—the event will get messier than a bulimic at a buffet.

Percentage of Population Affected: Everyone, everything, everywhere.

Eat this list:

THAT PLANET EATER THING BUCKET LIST

☐ We're aware that he was a doctor and not a dietitian, but be willing to mine the collected works of DeForest Kelly to see what insight he might have had regarding this predicament.

☐ Since the durned thing eats planets, don't get any bright ideas about making a carved-soap dummy replacement of yourself and trying to trick the Eater. Countless races have attempted tomfoolery such as this and failed.

☐ If Chuck Norris is still alive, get him to kick the Eater's ass.

☐ The Eater is allegedly quite a fan of that Seven of Nine gal from *Voyager*. You *know* she'll still be hot by 2028. Exert global peer pressure on her to stall the Eater by whatever (and we do mean *whatever*) means necessary.

☐ Encourage NASA to launch an enormous space platform that will reside next to Neptune with a brightly colored sign the size of China that reads: "Hi. We're Earth!" If the turd can be tricked into devouring a gas giant, it could cause him discomfort like a perro grande.

☐ Consider launching Dick Cheney directly into the eye of the beast. Ineffective? Maybe. Wildly entertaining? Absolutely!

☐ We bet that Dyson guy will have made huge advancements in vacuum technology by then. See if one of his fancy-shmancy vacuums can go toe-to-toe with the Eater.

☐ Ask the Eater if it would consider merely taking a sample and moving on.

☐ History will show that in the year 2025, Ryan Seacrest is the world's wealthiest man. Have him offer the turd a series on *E!*

The Grim Rating:

X marks nothing—3.1.

"Wow. I'll give it a bump for the devastation factor, but that's all. A huge letdown."

How It'll Go Down: Who knew? Apparently there's a tenth planet (we still count Pluto, thank you *very* much) in our solar system named Nibiru, which also answers to "Planet X." This wayward rock has an orbit that nearly intersects with Earth every 3,600 years or so, give or take a century. Historians tell us that on Nibiru's last visit, the gravitational effects of its proximity to Earth made Atlantis sink and gave the inhabitants of Shangri-La crabs.

If the math is right, our planet is due for another visit in the year 2012 and probably right around December, which will, once again, screw up holiday shopping. Nibiru, which is named for the Greek god of haute couture, will look stunning as it sashays through our solar system, coming within a frightening 5,000 miles of Earth and strutting its stuff as it moves on. See ya again in 3,600 years, girlfriend!

Estimated Length of Disaster: The best guess is seven to ten days. Since no legible records exist of Nibiru's previous visit (Atlanteans—an advanced race with pitiable penmanship), it's difficult to determine exactly what Planet X equals.

Percentage of Population Affected: It looks like only about 28–30% of the population. The damage to buildings and infrastructure will far surpass the human toll. The number of insurance claims will be overwhelming—most, however, will be rejected due to a lack of "Rogue Planet" coverage.

One list to rock the world:

NIBIRU BUCKET LIST

☐ Have Earth's retailers contact the Nibiruans and plead with them to delay the planet's pass-by until after the new year. Explain to the nomadic inhabitants that the holiday shopping season needs to be a biggie in order to make year-end bonuses. Sweeten the re-quest with a $500 gift card to Hickory Farms. (The Nibiruans love them some salami!)

☐ Hurricane Katrina was way too much for FEMA to handle, so don't expect much gov-ernment aid during this situation. A bottle of water and a coupon for a cookie might be as good as it gets.

☐ In a remarkable gesture of goodwill, ar-range for everyone on our world to simul-taneously wave at the Nibiruans as their planet reaches its closest point. Even if they don't wave back, keep waving. But please, no rainbow wigs.

☐ Can repulsor technology be perfected in time to counteract the gravitational effects? Or would a series of enormous blow-dryers be better? See what Tony Stark thinks (but *only* if he isn't hittin' the hooch).

☐ Use the flyby as an opportunity to send rockets filled with settlers to Nibiru, wipe out the indigenous life forms, and build condos.

☐ Create a space billboard to intercept Nibiru prior to its flyby. It will read: "It's only been 3,392 years! We're not dressed yet. Please come back later."

☐ How about you telekinetically gifted folks? Can you please band together and push that rock further away? We're all impressed with the fact that you can move a spoon with your mind, but aim higher, heroes.

☐ Research what info regarding Nibiru was entered into the Blessed Books of Shangri-La. Try not to get annoyed when you're reminded their sacred tomes are all in pop-up format.

☐ Pray that Earth and Nibiru don't get sweet on each other. Sure, our planet deserves a companion. It would, however, be better if it wasn't a huge mass that creates geological catastrophes. Love's a bitch, Earth. Get a dog.

Family of Blobs!

The Grim Rating:

Beyond abysmal—0.01.

"I can't say enough bad things about the Blobs. These a-holes have been disappointing in every outing. Now, if you'll excuse me, I'm going to have a good cry. And then go eviscerate their home planet."

How It'll Go Down: One of the Blob's kids decides it's going to get revenge on the State of Pennsylvania and the U.S. Air Force for defeating its dad decades ago. Blob Jr. convinces three of its cousins to join the mission, and together, they save up their allowances and buy a rickety craft that gets them to Earth. Sadly, the Blobs' navigation skills suck and instead of landing at their intended target of Philadelphia, they end up a fur piece away, outside the quiet Amish community of Bird-in-Hand.

This location proves to be very frustrating for the Blobs as, within a matter of days, they consume the entire town's population and their critters, leaving the Blobs with little to do but sit around and wait for the occasional busload of tourists to arrive.

The Blobs quickly become testy with one another, and they begin to bicker about what they should've done differently. One of the cousins goes too far and says that the original Blob (Blob Sr.) wasn't even that cool. After all, it's pointed out, the dad was defeated by an actor whose last name was McQueen. McQueen? Really?? From there, the hostilities escalate and a Blob equivalent to fisticuffs ensues, which is a grotesque thing to behold.

Estimated Length of Disaster*:* As soon as winter arrives, the Blobs are frozen and slip into suspended animation. Foolish Blobs.

Percentage of Population Affected: 0.000000000003%. A massive fail by the Blobs.

A misshapen list:

FAMILY OF BLOBS BUCKET LIST

☐ Arm the Amish with fire extinguishers. We know they might think it's too "modern," but tell 'em to get over it. Getting eaten by a Blob is also kinda modern. Do they want that?

☐ Contact the relatives of Steve McQueen and see if they want in on any of this action.

☐ Ask the Amish to explain what the deal is with not allowing belts. What are pants expected to do?

☐ If you happen to drop by Bird-in-Hand during what CNN will call the "Blobcupation" (and the Blobcupation logo will be underscored with a dark bluesy groove), stay at least fifteen feet away from the Blobs at all times. They may look like Wham-O products, but when they start to shimmy, run like hell.

☐ If you insist on staying in town, pay a visit to Sarah's Button Barn, where you'll find the most disturbing buttons you'd ever hope to see. Buttons made from mule heads and deer bones. Weird shit like that.

□ Helpful fact: ICEE is to Blob as crucifix is to vampire.

□ Y'know, that son-invades-a-foreign-place-to-get-revenge-on-behalf-of-his-dad scenario sounds familiar. Where the heck have we heard that before?

□ Retrieve the frozen father from the Arctic, thaw his Blob ass out, ship him to Pennsylvania, and reunite him with his family. Good karma all around!

Yorggh, the Biggest Damn Space Creature Ever!

The Grim Rating:

This schlemiel has to go—2.8.

"I do *not* enjoy having my death's work screwed with. From what I know of this Yorggh, he's incapable of doing *any* job correctly. I bet that due to his incompetence, my take will be meager. But hey, I'm willing to be surprised!"

How It'll Go Down: From beyond the stars comes Yorggh, the space creature so large that when he sits around the galaxy, he sits *around* the galaxy.

Yorggh fills the sky when he's as far away as the Moon. Why, his hat alone is as big as Saturn. Oh, right—it *is* Saturn.

Not known for his intellectual prowess, Yorggh more than makes up for it with his staggering size. He meanders aimlessly through the cosmos in search of splendid activities and edible stars. In his escapades, he frequently sideswipes planets, only noticing he ran into something well after the fact. If sound could be heard in space, this is what his reaction to a collision would be: "Whu?"

Think of Yorggh as a galactic version of Steinbeck's Lenny, and then imagine roughly 114.276 billion Lennys duct-taped together and packed into a gelatinous frozen form hundreds of thousands of miles across—at least during the cosmic holidays, what with all the overindulging at The Ringbelt All-You-Can-Eat.

In the winter of 2122, Yorggh will pass through our solar system. He'll initially have his middle eye on our Sun but will decide it's too small to be sweet. (Stars aren't like vegetables—the little ones frequently aren't tasty.)

Anyway, by the time Yorggh changes his mind about the Sun, he may have dinged multiple planets in our solar system, including Earth. Did we mention that Yorggh doesn't have liability insurance?

Estimated Length of Disaster: It's still up in the air about whether Yorggh will T-bone us. If he enters from the other side of the solar system, he'll be more likely to ding Jupiter. If, however, he comes in at an angle closer to the Sun, we could be screwed. And if that happens, it'll be over quickly. Like a matter of seconds. But, you know, if you've gotta go, that might be the way!

Percentage of Population Affected: From 0 to 100%.

The list:

YORGGH BUCKET LIST

☐ Remember: the *H* is silent in Yorggh. There's no cumulative *F* sound there. And it's not Yiddish either.

☐ Is Alison Sweeney available to speak to Yorggh about his size? Isn't it time for Yorggh to think about cutting back on his carb intake? Does he have a death wish or merely eating issues? What's the emotional hole he's trying to fill?

☐ If Yorggh approaches our planet, get everyone to yell, "HEY, LOOK OUT!"

☐ Speak to The Planetary Council Guys about installing Planetary Air Bags, just to be on the safe side.

☐ Encourage the Oort Cloud to step up to the plate and run interference.

☐ Has Yorggh heard about the wonders of these powdered shakes we're selling? They'll transform his life.

☐ That's right. These shakes contain a patented protein formula that will help melt away whole sectors from Yorggh's body. This could extend Yorggh's life by centuries. Easily.

☐ Is there a Mrs. Yorggh? Wouldn't she appreciate it if her manly space creature looked more like the thing she met a millennium ago? These shakes mix easily with water and become a delicious meal substitute.

☐ No, really—we'll give Yorggh the starter kit for free if he'll promise to commit to the Ninety-Year Challenge.

Earth Ejects Its Own Core!

The Grim Rating:

That's more like it—10!!

"I've wanted to eff up that Gaia skank forever. I'm gonna savor this!"

How It'll Go Down: Pity our poor planet. About a century from now, it gets way bummed about its own condition. After all, one can only take so many hurricanes, earthquakes, and tornadoes; the collective carnage is overwhelming. And it's not like humans are helping—overpopulation and unchecked pollution will have left the Earth in horrible shape, flabby, and with an equatorial spare tire.

In responding, the planet will take matters into its own "hands" and decide it can't go on like this. In a monumental feat worthy of a Michael Bay film, our beloved globe will poop out its own core, which will rise to the ocean's surface not far from New Zealand and stink up the joint. As

a result of the core's ejection, the planet will slow in its orbit and start to break apart, which will no doubt address that overpopulation problem.

Estimated Length of Disaster: A matter of days. But we'll say this—if you're all about disasters, these will be fun days!

Percentage of Population Affected: It's the *planet*, ya goomba. Everyone's going down!

Here's your poopy list:

EARTH EJECTS OWN CORE BUCKET LIST

☐ By knowing that the Earth will develop emotional issues down the road, do all you can every day to tell it you love it. Kiss a tree, hug the dirt, anything.

☐ Once a week, visit your backyard and work a bag of shredded sharp cheddar cheese into the soil. It can be quite binding and, over time, may help prevent core poopage. (And who doesn't love cheese?)

☐ No matter what incentive package Peter Jackson offers you, do *not* move to New Zealand!

☐ See if Dr. Drew is willing to donate his time into talking the planet down from the ledge of tomorrow.

☐ If you happen to be reading this and it's still the twenty-first century, perhaps you'll take comfort in the fact that this won't impact you—only your grandchildren and their kids. It's *their* problem and that's what they get for never writing thank-you notes for the various gifts you've sent. Ingrates.

☐ Start a campaign to get the world's governments to fund a mission that would send a manned vehicle into the Earth to pinpoint the planet's poop hole and plug it. Design bitchin' Dirt-O-Naut suits with a sort of prospector-chic look.

☐ Hire one of them medium gals with the ESP to make contact with Gaia the Earth Goddess on your behalf. When you get the Spirit O' The Planet on the line, lay down the honey. Start the chat with a dash of flattery and tell her she looks her best in the morning; that'll get you brownie points. Remind Gaia that she's still in her prime. Tell her she needs to stop using Botox—her lips appear flubberish.

☐ Speaking of solving the overpopulation problem, maybe consider not having that *fourteenth* child or a reality TV show about your reproductive ambitions. You're bumming the world out.

☐ Even though the event is a century away, start justifying new strange behaviors and pricey purchases with this phrase: "Hey, if the world's gonna end, I'm gonna live a little." Maybe a new snake?

☐ Reduce your carbon footprint to something even the Wallendas wouldn't walk on.

Historically Large Solar Flare Scorches the Globe!

The Grim Rating:

A middling 7.1.

"If a damn G2V star isn't good for more than a single X-Class flare, then, sister, I'm livin' in the wrong universe! Where's the justice, I ask you?"

How It'll Go Down: Cosmic in scale, hence its presence here.

The Sun will wake up one day in a particularly cranky mood, feeling extra sensitive about how much plasma it's been retaining. In a huff, it'll decide to drop some tonnage.

Straining, as if it's trying to pinch a solar loaf, the Sun will jettison a historically huge flare, definitely an X-Class that flames harder than Carson Kressley. When that flare reaches us, it will encircle the entire

world. The axis of our planet will become a rotisserie of sorts, basting the Earth in its atmospheric juices.

With luck, this single blast will provide sufficient relief to the frustrated Sun so that no more will be necessary. If the Sun ends up squeezing off additional flares of that magnitude, we're toast. Burnt toast.

Estimated Length of Disaster: Let's see: Eight minutes for a flare to reach the Earth and anything more than a day on the rotisserie. You do the math.

Percentage of Population Affected: 73.3%. The most northerly regions will fare best. Bless your Nordic hearts!

This list is burning a hole in our pockets:

SOLAR FLARE BUCKET LIST

☐ SPF 12,000.

☐ Tailor-made sunshade three-piece suit. It's silvery *and* stylish!!

☐ Immediately dump your interest in the tanning salon chain U Look Sunsational. Invest those profits into B-stock air conditioners and sell those babies when the prices skyrocket.

☐ If ever there were a reason to leave the San Fernando Valley, this would be it. Or Needles. Or Yuma. *Especially* Yuma.

☐ If you live in the extreme northern or southern latitudes, prepare for a rapid thaw—an inflatable-raft level of thaw.

☐ Build an awesome subterranean clubhouse. Buy one-hundred-foot extension cords to be strung from the generator inside the fireproof shed. Get a mini-fridge, a microwave, and a smoking jacket. Do *not* invite your stupid neighbor over who goes on and on about his friend's kid who claims he's going to be on *X Factor*. We've heard him "sing"—it's not gonna happen.

☐ Adjust solar panels for maximum absorption. Watch kilowatt wheel spin backward like Michele Kwan.

☐ If you're still alive by the end of the first flare, check out the evening sky. Make Grateful Dead playlist and try to score 'shrooms for the Aurora Borealis!

☐ Should you choose to venture outdoors, you'll not only be able to fry eggs on the sidewalk, but entire chickens too. Solar Flare Block Party BBQ. Yes!!

☐ Internet speeds will suck dramatically and/or be down due to lingering electromagnetic issues. For Blackberry users, it'll be business as usual.

Galactus!

The Grim Rating:

This dude is a 10!

"I've been hot to trot for that hunky Big G for ages. He's the rare combination of looks and smarts, strong and silent. And I, for one, admire a cosmic force that continues to pursue his dreams after thousands of years. Call me, G-Dog!"

How It'll Go Down: You'll be relieved to know that Galactus—a devourer of worlds and a guy who pulls off purple better than Prince—won't arrive as an insipid swirling cloud as he was portrayed in that smelly Fantastic Four flick. No, this will be the *real* Galactus, complete with his unnecessarily ornate helmet, tacky tunic, and standing about three hundred feet tall (*much* bigger than what Marvel says) with a giant *G* on his chest. As usual, he'll be interested

in feeding on our world, and there won't be an actual Reed Richards or Silver Surfers to save us this time.

You heard correctly—Galactus is legit, and as we've been warned, once he sets up shop on a given planet, he breaks out his planet-sucking contraption. This thing is akin to a huge wet-dry vac that inhales the life force from the globe, which Galactus then chugs like a freshman at his first kegger. (Think "Earth shooters.") The absence of the life-force leaves the populace leathery and feeble, resembling members of a Palm Springs shuffleboard club. And then the whole planet croaks.

Estimated Length of Disaster: From the time Galactus lands until the time he flicks the three-story-tall on/off switch, it'll be a matter of days. That is, unless someone can convince him that we're a noble race and deserve to be spared. Yeah, right.

Percentage of Population Affected: That would be everyone. What part of "devourer of worlds" eludes you?

Devour this list!

GALACTUS BUCKET LIST

☐ Invent the Ultimate Nullifier, wave it at Galactus, and yell, "Yoo-hoo! Oh, Mr. Geeeee! Look who's got an Ultimate Nullifier!"

☐ Ask that damn Watcher to stop being such a voyeuristic skeeve and take some action!

☐ Design a PowerPoint presentation demonstrating the goodness of humanity and why we should survive. Avoid any bullet points referencing these deeds: the Holocaust, the Crusades, the McCarthy Era, the settling of the Old West, the Salem Witch Trials, the sex trade, whaling, the genocide in Darfur, slavery, Apple's factory conditions in China, and anything that involves the manner in which animals are mistreated every day.

☐ Put together an ad campaign aimed at Galactus's demographic that promotes Venus as a more nutritious planet.

☐ Superglue Galactus's feet to the ground so that if he devours us, he gets consumed too. Good one, huh?

☐ Arrange for a gaggle of comedy writers to gather at his feet and insult him for hours. This would be like a celebrity roast, but with no show of love at the end. (And without Andy Dick.) Have the comics make fun of his clothes, his helmet, his trouser snake, his family, the giant *G*—nothing's off limits. The goal: Have Galactus go running home in tears.

☐ Trip him with a stick and, while he's down, pull off his helmet and repeatedly elbow his skull. Make him tap out.

☐ Convince Galactus that he needs a permit to operate his planet-draining machine, and until such time as he obtains one, he's forbidden to operate the device. And then—this is the important part—make sure no one *ever* issues him a permit!

Part 3

The Invasions:
Who Invited *Them*?

Robots!

The Grim Rating:

Squeeee! 9.5.

"The drag here, darlings, is robots don't count as souls. However, their efficiency in polishing *you* off sure cuts down on my work. I guess robots really *are* time-savers!!!"

How It'll Go Down: It'll happen in the spring, when cherry blossoms are sweet and life begins anew. A shuttered auto assembly plant in Detroit will find a way to bring itself online and start creating new workers from scratch. (It misses the company, so to speak.)

As the robot workers duplicate, they spread their operations to other nearby deserted plants. During this time, they also manage to manufacture a sentient and adorable little two-seater convertible. Ya gotta hand it to 'em—they're productive.

As they perfect their replication processes, they become bored (and short on parts) and decide that human organs and tissues will add a bit of bling to their mechanical brethren.

And so, the war will begin. No mechanical device will ever again be trustworthy, except for levers and pulleys, who'll sit this one out. Even blenders will be suspect. The machine takeover will be brutal, but not to worry—you may get to come back as part of a hybrid human-robot package. At least your life will have a purpose.

Estimated Length of Disaster: This disaster will take a good, long while. The robots are efficient, but that's a lot of zeroes and ones to be crunched.

Percentage of Population Affected: Gosh, over time, everyone. Sad, right?

Here's your list, fleshy human meat sack:

ROBOT INVASION BUCKET LIST

☐ Stock up on WD-40 for "Welcome, Mechanical Overlords" gift baskets.

☐ Become more expressive in your affection for your appliances, going so far as to curtsy to the toaster.

☐ Stop assuming your car wants to parallel park your lazy ass. Instead, start asking if *it* wants to go on field trips.

☐ Make sure you're watching *Terminator* and cheering for the machines when the SecuriBots arrive.

☐ Visit the nearest ocean one last time before it's converted into pure hydrogen for the aforementioned overlords.

☐ Listen to the "Surrender and/or Die" podcast your iPod downloaded for you without your permission.

☐ Consider the luddite lifestyle.

☐ Don't trust your panic room. It doesn't have your best interests at heart.

☐ Attend the Overlord Job Fair held by the Robot High Command. Entertain the idea of pursuing new careers such as Second-Shift Polisher, Lubricant Manager Trainee, or Skin Donation Attendant.

☐ Contact Col. Steve Austin and see what his input/output is.

The Return of the Mayans!

The Grim Rating:

Mayans, shmayans—3.2.

"While I appreciate the sacrificial offerings, the rest of their efforts are weak. More vengeance, less posing, I say. Get your golden butts to Spain and work some magic!"

How It'll Go Down: We say "Mayans," you say "Doomsday!" "Mayans!" "_____!"

In the summer of 2016, a series of sparkly, blue beams o' light will appear in the sky over Central America. As those bright beams find their way to Earth, striking humanoids will emerge from the indigo glow. Their skin will be gold and their cheekbones exquisite. They'll appear to have been dressed by a designer heavily influenced by Bob Mackie *and* Spartacus. These warriors/models will reveal themselves to be the descendants of the Mayans. They'll claim they've been living in another dimension for centuries, perfecting their minds and bodies while taking nifty crafts classes. They'll also announce they've returned to reclaim their homeland.

The conquest will start in Guatemala and work its way through the region. Not surprisingly, there will be little resistance because of how freakin' cool these Mayans are—like a bunch of hopped-up Khans (*Trek*, not Genghis). Local dictators will, put up a fight as the Mayan forces cross into their countries. However, in one dramatic circumstance, the Mayan leader, Quetzalganoush, will wave his hand and a despot's head will launch from his neck like a champagne cork. This'll make the Mayans even more beloved.

These otherworldly hotties will seek to conquer only one other place—Spain. The Mayans *really* know how to hold a grudge.

Estimated Length of Disaster: Kinda hard to actually define this as a disaster unless you're a tyrant. True, this change will wreak havoc on the resort industry, but the Mayans will rule over most of Central America and Spain with a firm and loving hand. We'll give 'em a mulligan on the human sacrifices.

Percentage of Population Affected: 6% maybe. Most of the world will think, "As long as it doesn't happen to me or mine."

Bow to the list:

MAYANS BUCKET LIST

☐ Those Mayans are going to want to maintain their golden hue in our dimension. This might be the right time to sink your savings into a spray-on tan business in Belize.

☐ Quetzalganoush will be establishing a network of lackeys and a harem. The more you can aid him, the less chance of being one of the sacrifices.

☐ There will be an urgent need for gold. If you're in one of their targeted areas, melt whatever you have and drop it off (with a nice note) at any conveniently placed Gold Collection Station.

☐ A franchise of Mayan Temples might also take off in this new environment. One-stop shopping for worship and sacrifices!

☐ Since the Yucatan Peninsula will also belong to the Mayans, schedule a farewell trip to Cancun before it falls. It won't be as upbeat afterward—fewer paper umbrellas.

☐ Unwieldy flamboyant helmets will be back in vogue, so wear 'em if you've got 'em.

☐ Do the Mayans accept substitutions re: the sacrifices? Discuss the possibility of replacing humans with mannequins. No muss, no fuss, no screaming. And cleanup, by comparison, is a snap!

☐ Don't confuse the Mayans with Incans or Aztecs—it makes them snappish.

That Flying Turtle Fella with Flames Comin' Out of His Butt!

The Grim Rating:

And I thought the Blobs were bad—0.001.

"This is an event that'll barely surface on my radar. Figures—a flying turtle whose name can't be remembered. Lowers the bar in a multitude of ways. This is the type of 'disaster' that makes it hard to get out of bed some mornings."

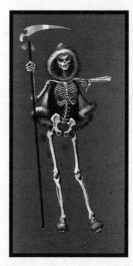

How It'll Go Down: How would *you* like to be a monster whose name nobody remembers? That would tweak you, wouldn't it? No wonder this turtle's got fire comin' out of his butt!

So Camera or Carbonara or whatever its name is will show up in Japan as it does every few decades. Everyone will be horrified, but no one will know (or remember) what to call it. This makes for awkward news stories and scores of befuddled water-cooler conversations. Citizens will point to the sky in terror and say "Look, it's uhhhhhhh…" and then start giggling. Because of this, Cantina or Bugari will get crankier, spin around, do the flaming butt trick, and take out most of downtown Tokyo. (All monsters *know* that if you want to make the right impression, destroying part of downtown Tokyo is essential.)

After having blown his flaming-turtle wad, the cantankerous ecotherm will spin and hover for a while admiring his handiwork. By the end of Day Ten, the populace will have become bored with the entire deal. Seeing this, the turtle throws has a snit and leaves, destined to return to whatever depressing no-name home he has—probably some shitty cave.

Estimated Length of Disaster: A couple of weeks and that'll be all his flaming butt wrote. This is a candy-ass disaster by any standard.

Percentage of Population Affected: Less than 1%, if that. Not much more than part of downtown Tokyo. What's that—like 100 million?

A list that serves as a cheap opportunity to say "flaming butt trick" one last time:

FLYING TURTLE BUCKET LIST

☐ Don't let the turtle hear you not get his name right. (*Awkward.*) That can set him off. If you have to come up with his name in his presence, fake a cough or a spasm when talking. That might let you off the hook and minimize your chances of becoming a pile of ashes.

☐ Not to state the obvious but, because this one's *so* location-centric, staying in Tokyo would be a poor decision, unless you happen to live in the suburbs fifty or sixty miles from the area the turtle always trashes.

☐ Camaro? Panera? Gilgamesh?

☐ Just because those flames are coming out of his butt, don't think it's funny. (Well, sure it is from a distance, but not if you're there and on fire.)

☐ For everyone who *doesn't* live in Japan, assemble considerate care packages for the citizens of Tokyo. That way, you'll experience less guilt about your "Burn Tokyo" watch parties.

☐ Carnita? Gamboni? Jabberwock?

☐ One of these decades somebody needs to come up with a way to either kill the turtle or ask him not to return. Rebuilding sections of downtown Tokyo every thirty years or so is getting spendy.

☐ If you actually try to fight back, aim a water cannon at his posterior. You might put out his pilot light.

☐ All you other Asian nations—you know who you are—don't get a kick out of the misfortune of the Japanese. You never know when you might get a turtle of your own with its own brand of—wait for it—flaming butt trick. (Ding!)

☐ Gargantua? Gerbera? Gamera?

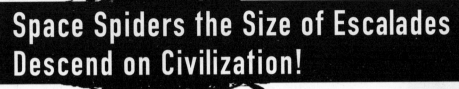

Space Spiders the Size of Escalades Descend on Civilization!

The Grim Rating:

Unacceptable—5.8.

"Even *I* hate spiders! If I find one in my bachelorette pad, I usually call S'tan to come squish it for me."

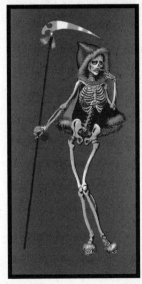

How It'll Go Down: GE's Large Scale Satellite for No Publicly Released Reason to Exist will fail in its orbit a mere two months after its launch. Like Patsy Cline, it will fall to pieces. The largest piece, which will land outside of Truth or Consequences, New Mexico, will have hitchhikers aboard. On that hunk of top-secret junk, there will be five small space spiders. (They were attracted to the warmth the satellite provided and found the object to be a great fit for their active lifestyles.)

After landing and being exposed to our environment, these spiders will grow and reproduce in a major way, like Duggars (whose scenario comes later). These suckers will spawn and grow at an astounding rate. Within days, five become sixty become seven thousand. Bottom line—*we're* what's for dinner.

Estimated Length of Disaster: These spiders could take up to a year to completely dominate the boards, but the result isn't a done deal. There's a slight chance of survival if we start building silo-sized cans of Raid now!

Percentage of Population Affected: This one's tough—if we lose the war, most everyone will be wrapped in silk except for folks on certain islands that the spiders couldn't reach. (Personal note from the gang here at The Lists: people who live on islands piss us off. Where do they *get off* living on an island?! It seems elitist to us and a way by which to avoid all sorts of responsibility.) Even if we win the war, we still may lose about 52% of the population.

Here's your creepy-crawly list:

SPACE SPIDERS BUCKET LIST

☐ This begs the question: What would Peter Parker do?

☐ Land mine the lawn.

☐ Snakes and spiders are mortal enemies, or at least that's what Billy Jim the salesman at The Reptile Roundup said. That's the great new store by you that used to be a Denny's and has since become a snake collector's dream. Billy Jim says now's the time to take up the hobby. Spring for that boa you've been admiring! And if you're going to take the plunge, then—what the heck—get the albino one.[1]

☐ Install exceptionally large magnifying glass on roof and fry those spiders when they hit your 'hood.

1. Owning snakes can be dangerous—this book accepts no responsibility for your actions. If snake collecting ends up causing you problems, direct your anger at Billy Jim and Reptile Roundup, Inc, and *not* at us.

☐ Who cares what we said earlier? Move to an island ASAP! I hear Fiji is fabu.

☐ When the eight-legged devils are bearing down on you, bathe yourself in insecticide. You may still get wrapped, but the chemicals will screw them up!

☐ Stock up on rats. That boa is *hungry!*

☐ And don't answer the phone when Billy Jim the salesman calls. He's going to try to press you into buying another boa. He'll say, "Your snake needs a buddy." He'll pause briefly and then add, "And you know those spiders are comin'.".

☐ Bask in the fact that you now own two boas and your security concerns are solved. Hold it—are they mating?

Werewolves!

The Grim Rating:

Doggone it—4.5.

"It's hard to take a disaster seriously when its instigators respond to the word 'sit.' Yes, they're fierce and vicious, but they're easily distracted by tennis balls."

How It'll Go Down: Oddly enough, it'll be the Westminster Kennel Club Dog Show that will trigger the werewolf population's assault on mankind. In a well-coordinated attack, thousands of lycanthropes will pour out of the sublevels of Madison Square Garden and into the arena, after having knocked out power to the building. They'll make short work of the poor, befuddled, overdressed crowd. As a choir of howls is heard, the show dogs will join in the fray, responding to the primal call. The fanciest poodles with simply the cutest cuts will turn on their

handlers and rip out the throats and ankles of as many humans as they can reach. Oh, there *will* be leg humping, but of the fatal variety.

Estimated Length of Disaster: The Dog Show Disaster will only last one evening but will be the first volley in the werewolves' effort to make their presence known. No more living in darkness or fear for them. And no more of that crappy generic kibble.

Percentage of Population Affected: Very difficult to say. The werewolf agenda will be unclear. One minute they'll be claiming the planet, the next they're chasing bunnies. For an ancient species, they sure have focus issues.

Ah-ooooooooo (that's a howling sound):

WEREWOLVES BUCKET LIST

☐ If you own an obedience school, shutter it.

☐ Enlist the aid of Cesar Milan. His "whisper-ing" may not stop the attacks, but maybe the 'wolves will be less brutal. Better a couple of shallow bites than having your ass ripped off.

☐ Keep in mind that there will still be no an-tidote for the virus that the lycanthropes transmit. If you survive the initial attack, you'll want to get used to the concepts of sniffing butts and eating unidentifiable items off the lawn.

☐ Arm yourself and your loved ones with squeeze toys and pig ears. These may distract the werepups long enough for you to escape.

☐ Encourage your own dogs to place their paw prints on a loyalty oath and have such oath notarized. Remind the dogs on a daily basis that you expect them to honor their word (or bark or whatever the equivalent is).

☐ Also, should you happen to be one of those troglodytes that operates a puppy mill, you're destined to be a Milk-Bone.

☐ A prominent scientist believes that, once the werewolves surface, this will bring forth the hidden race of Cat People. This development will lead to lots of commotion in alleyways and a perpetual ruckus out your back window.

☐ Once the canine conquerors emerge, *all* parks will become dog parks and no one will be cleaning up their poop. Start throwing your Frisbees elsewhere.

☐ "Who's a good boy" will avail you naught.

Return of the Dinosaurs!

The Grim Rating:

I like 'em big and dumb—8.6!

"Woot! Sometimes a gal just needs giant lizards to make her life—uh, death—a little easier. Bless their pea brains!"

How It'll Go Down: While a natural gas company is merrily fracking in southern Alberta, one of its crews will blow open a passage leading deep into the Earth. This tunnel will connect to a subterranean world—a place where dinosaurs frolic freely. (Well, frolic may be a stretch.) This land is a dim and magical place where no mini malls exist. (Though I'm sure we'll get around to correcting that.)

It will be theorized that the great beasts long ago sought refuge underground after another zany comet struck the Earth. Scientists believe that once the unwieldy creatures became comfortable with the limited light, they forgot about the surface world. This may have to do with the fact that their brains are the size of walnuts. (It's been said that even the Bill Gates of the dinosaur community had a brain no bigger than a kiwi fruit.)

When the passage is reopened, the dinosaurs will smell the light (this is not a form of synesthesia—that's how their senses work) and they'll have a collective "oh yeah" moment. Once they reach the surface, it'll get all kinds of ugly quick-like. The fresh air and sunshine will breathe new life into them and out of us.

Estimated Length of Disaster: We don't mean to hang it all on the G.I. Joes and Janes, but realistically, the solution *will* probably fall to the military strategists and soldiers of whatever countries respond. A matchup we like: stealth bombers against pterodactyls! Nice air show, huh? If the world's troops can't get a handle on these vicious artifacts, we'll be screwed. Within a year, mankind will no longer be considered the "dominant species," and our credit rating will surely suffer.

Percentage of Population Affected: Unless aggressively countered, this could be a disaster that hovers in the upper ninetieth percentile. Only those in the higher altitudes will be spared.

Your lumbering lizard list:

DINOSAURS BUCKET LIST

☐ Some of the dinosaurs are herbivores, you know. Don't start screaming like a little girl just because a brontosaurus shows up in your backyard. It's not the end of the world. Offer it your garden and slowly back away.

☐ The T-Rex is everything they say and more. Put aluminum foil over the windows and Lysol your house to eliminate as much of your personal odor as possible. They can see your stench.

☐ As for the raptors, they're quite vicious. Having said that, we believe any parent who's dealt with a two-year-old will be prepared to encounter a raptor. Not unlike your own screaming tot, raptors can't be reasoned with and would prefer hysteria rather than genuine discourse. Behavioral specialists agree—a firm scolding or time-out may teach the raptorish ruffians (and your child) the same valuable lesson.

☐ When all of the beasts leave their subterranean lair, pull a fast one on those prehistoric pinheads and sneak down there with your family. Close the cave behind you.

☐ Find a comet or asteroid (petite, if possible) to strike the part of the planet with the most dinosaurs. Did they learn *nothing*?

☐ Round 'em up and put soaring electrified fences around 'em as a sort of scientific game preser—oh. Never mind.

☐ Another location that might be relatively safe: anywhere bitterly cold. Four out of five dentists claim that most dinosaurs simply abhor the frostier temps as they continue to deal with emotional matters remaining from the Ice Age. (Why dentists are expressing opinions about the psychological states of dinosaurs is hard for us to understand.) Anyway, find yourself a frozen chunk of horrible land and call it home!

☐ Plan your vacations around the times when the military will be making their monthly stands. These shows should not be missed! Get in on these eco-dinowar-tour junkets if you can. They're usually wallet friendly!

☐ Feed Barney to a T-Rex. "I love you, you love me, ACKrrghhhhh!" Crunch. Nice.

Those Pod Things! You Know, Those *Pod* Things!

The Grim Rating:

Boooooooring—5.0.

"You wouldn't believe the hoops I had to jump through to put that thought in ex-Prez Bingo's head about buying his boy a seat on that mission. I swear, when it comes to the dude's mind, there's no there, there."

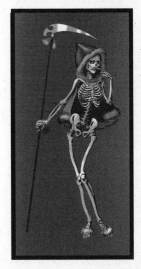

How It'll Go Down: In 2032, the first human will step onto the surface of Venus. Fortunately, the landing site will be the one place near the North Pole where it's not 240 degrees all the damn time. The landing will be a proud moment for mankind but will leave Venus feeling violated.

While exploring the planet, Commander Dutch Bingo Jr., the first astronaut to ever have his passage on a spaceship bought by his dad, will discover a tiny field of plants with thick hanging orange pods. Stupidly, he picks the pods like they're crab apples and totes them back to the craft. During Junior's pod show-and-tell with his fellow 'nauts, a mist is released by the pods that smells a lot like that leftover furry blue chili in the back of our fridge here at The Lists. Stanky.

The mysterious mist will turn the hapless crew into slaves, enabling the pods to gain control of the crew's minds, which in the case of Bingo, Jr. nets the pods little.

These "Venusian Man-Traps" will telepathically order the spacemen to return to Earth, where the pods believe they can do to our planet what they've done to the crew. NASA will not be able to grok the crew's poor communication with ground control and why such chatter's been reduced to "uh-huhs" and "uh-uhs." This behavior is eventually attributed to what's known in the astronaut game as "Apollo Apathy," a condition by which, over time, the human mind becomes numb to the majesty of space and, instead, craves the comfort of bad TV.

Once the crew and the Man-Traps arrive, the pods will spread like crazy, turning once-vibrant citizens into glassy-eyed sheep. The ratings for *Dancing with the Stars* will soar.

Estimated Length of Disaster: Unless a cure can be found for the mist, this could continue for quite some time.

Percentage of Population Affected: We can't know this—we only know what the pods tell us.

Inhale deeply and we'll read you the list:

THOSE POD THINGS BUCKET LIST

☐ Find a way to make sure that President Bingo never reproduces. Or even has sex. (Ew.)

☐ Don't talk to pods or anyone in their thrall. Any form of interaction is highly discouraged.

☐ Certain scientists claim that by taking Benadryl, the mist's effects will be minimized. In other words, you won't be a complete slave but may be open to suggestions about who to vote for in the upcoming Pod Party elections.

☐ Speaking of Benadryl, apparently the pods have a host of allergy issues, which cause them to over-mist in the spring. Avoid pods at all times, but especially during this season—they can be pushier than normal and will try to get you to sign one of their petitions or take a stupid survey.

☐ Always wear a surgical mask. The look might be creepy, but better creepy than misted.

□ It doesn't matter who's on *DWTS* this week—do you really want to be part of that demographic now? C'mon. Pods and their slaves watch that!

□ Resist the urge to buy cookies from pods during their annual drive.

□ Again, the pods may attempt to telepathically chat you up and get you to talk about yourself. Keep in mind that no matter how personable they may seem, they're dead set on turning you into a slave.

□ It would be better if you didn't introduce a pod to your spouse or friends. These things have no sense of boundaries.

□ Do not allow a pod to sell you whole-term life insurance.

Vampires!

The Grim Rating:

A frustrating 6.

"Vampires chafe my scythe. They're like double jeopardy to me—I can only claim a being once and then they're off limits. I find vamps to be little more than pasty pests, except when they're pitching in on my behalf. Hey, anything to cut down on the workload. I'm no spring chicken, you know!"

How It'll Go Down: It turns out that vampires *do* exist and aren't nearly as glamorous or dreamy as we'd been led to believe. They are, in fact, grody and covered in what would appear to be dried blood. And painfully skinny too. How the hell did they ever get such a sexy rep? They must have terrific PR agents.

On a random night, sometime soon, we'll discover their real nature.

Their lifestyles have been frugal at best, picking off a lone human every so often so as not to be noticed. Like Native Americans with a buffalo, they used every bit of the human, even the navel lint to make plush coffin liners.

Over time, vampires' situations became more complicated—a population increase and a battle with an ongoing disease in their species changed their unlives. Because of these factors, they hunger incessantly. And the more they feed, the greater their numbers become. Thus, the greater the competition for remaining food. (That would be us.)

Estimated Length of Disaster: Impossible to know. Will their disease kill them or will it, as scientists speculate, instead take away their sensitivity to sunlight? Suffice it to say that wouldn't be the neatest development for the human race. As for the length, call it—the result is a coin in the air.

Percentage of Population Affected: We just told you it's impossible to know. What the heck?!

Here's your bloody list:

VAMPIRES BUCKET LIST

☐ Head to your nearby Apotropaic Symbols Superstore (don't use the acronym) and stock up on garlic bulbs, hawthorn branches, holy water, and all the other top sellers. Check out the sale on rosaries in Aisle 9! C'mon down and shop so you *don't* drop!

☐ And you gals, the vampires are, in reality, not interested in (A) your tatas, (B) your pouty red lips, or (C) your sophomoric romantic longings. You're nothing more than a bag of plasma to them. Sorry—it's better that you know now.

☐ Crossbows will only be effective if you're firing crucifixes. They sure do look butch though, don't they?

☐ You know that myth about spilling a pound of salt in front of a vampire and he'll have to count the grains? Well, we didn't know about it either. Anyway, we researched it—it's bogus and can get you killed. (Speaking of which, we'd like to extend our sympathies to the family of Jerry Farner, who was part of our team here at The Lists. He passed away while in service to this company. We miss ya, Jer! Skeeter bless.)

☐ Assuming that their disease doesn't endow the vamps with an immunity to sunlight, purchase a couple dozen of those anti-Seasonal Affective Disorder natural-light lamps and crank 'em up in your man cave. Once you're surrounded by that kind of wavelength, you should be gold.

☐ Remember: they're more *Nosferatu*-y than *Twilight*-y.

☐ If you're able to fight back, cut off an attacking vamp's head and remove said head from the body's location. Otherwise (and we've seen this happen), that dopey body is going to flop around like a trout on a dock and begin looking for its head. While it sounds like a hoot, furniture could get broken or fine stemware trashed during the thrashing.

☐ Helpful hint: Throw the severed head over your fence and into your stupid neighbor's backyard. Watch the fun ensue!

☐ Stop giving blood—you're going to need yours. Besides, the Red Cross is going to become merely a front for the vampires, part of their international storage network.

☐ Hang more crosses around your neck than that emo hippie inked-up biker magician feller that's jumped the shark. Ya know—what's his name.

Reptilux, the Ginormous Alien Lizard!

The Grim Rating:

A trifling 1.7.

"The dinosaurs were *great*, but this fifty-four-foot lizard should be faring better. The problem: he's all talk. He's so caught up in his *supposed* celebrity status, that he's lost his commitment to doing the hard work. Someday, I'm going to make a pair of bitchin' boots out of his lazy, fat ass."

How It'll Go Down: Reptilux is a fifty-four-foot lizard who's the Andrew Zimmern of space monsters. He travels extensively, reporting back to his native planet about the different places he's seen and eaten. He's considered a celebrity on multiple worlds.

While working on an episode, he'll breeze through our quadrant and decide that he should do a feature on Earth. While here, he'll discover

that, while he *does* savor the taste of the pink city apes, he also enjoys the mouth-feel of poorly constructed office buildings. He comes to the conclusion that a densely populated strip mall is like a sublime club sandwich and gives it three thumbs up.

The Lux, as he's called, needs to eat twice his weight each day in order to survive the rigors of space and, of course, to accurately sample the planet's fare. Within the first two days, his menu includes Cleveland and Cincinnati. One must wonder where he puts it all because he sure doesn't have much of a gut, especially for a lizard.

Estimated Length of Disaster: With any luck, he'll only chow down on Ohio and exit the arena. His show's budget doesn't allow him to spend much time on any one planet, so he works quickly, everything in one take.

Percentage of Population Affected: This may only be 10 to 20 million. We can afford that!

Your lizard list:

REPTILUX BUCKET LIST

☐ Check the Lux's backside and make sure there isn't a hidden zipper there with a mad genius inside working the controls.

☐ Arrange for the Lux to meet the Kardashians.

☐ Speak to the Jewel of Avia and summon HawkMo the Hell Bird to smite the Lux where he stands. Take note that this fight will be part of a bigger card that could include one other fight between a derivative monster and an irrelevant animal spirit.

☐ Comfort Ohio by reminding it that it'll be prominently featured in Reptilux's Earth episode.

☐ Speaking of derivative, research if the Lux is in copyright violation regarding Godzilla and intellectual property rights relating thereto. The Lux does *not* want Godzilla's legal team (Iguana & Goldberg) coming after him!

☐ See if Rodin is available. Oh crap, that's the sculptor. Sorry. See if Rodan is available.

☐ Discourage the Food Network from making overtures to the Lux regarding a show. Explain that it needs to do the math: higher ratings will lead to fewer viewers.

☐ Speak with the Gecko (perhaps it can offer insight) or Donald Trump.

☐ Boycott the companies whose ads run on the Lux's program. Don't buy Tentacle Helper or SmegLoaf.

Aliens!

The Grim Rating:

Survey says—9.0!

"I've never been much of a multitasker, so I'll allow the aliens to take you out and then I'll take *them* out. I love it when things come together so neatly!"

How It'll Go Down: The aliens are so boorish. They'll wait for a searingly hot North American summer day and show up in their massive, showy spaceships that just reek of an "Oh, we're soooooooooooo powerful" 'tude. They make ya wanna puke.

As fate would have it, we'll learn that the aliens *are* actually little green men, but a pleasant '80s shade of seafoam green. On land, they cruise around in bulky armored suits, overcompensating in ways we don't care to think about. The emerald organisms will explain that

their race has been lingering above our world for decades, studying our bizarre customs and looking down the blouses of our Earth women. It turns out they need our world for a science project and would appreciate it if they could exterminate 90% of us—the remaining 10% to be used as service workers, most of whom will need to wear go-go outfits. It gets better: they like our taste. No, you nimrod—not our *aesthetic* taste; they like *how* we taste, as in eating us. Get it now?

Estimated Length of Disaster: This invasion will last far longer than it needs to, due mainly to the aliens' need to properly document everything for their bloated bureaucracy.

Percentage of Population Affected: Approximately 85%. The little green suckas aren't interested in the colder regions of the planet. Consequently, places such as Iceland, Greenland, North Dakota, and Maine are safe. And Yellowknife—you're sittin' pretty, babe! How often do you Yellowknifians (??) get to hear that?

Take this list to your leader:

ALIEN INVASION BUCKET LIST

☐ If you choose to join the Resistance, buy a cool hat. An eye patch is slammin' too. Remember: everyone in the Resistance needs to look awesome. Don't be the lone non-looker.

☐ Feeling anxious about these aliens? Then why *wait* to be exterminated? Get it over with! Stop by any of the conveniently located Disintegration Kiosks, use the Express Lane (twelve humans or less), and ask for the "Pain-Free Package." Tell 'em we sent you!

☐ If you choose to volunteer for the Alien Service Corps, no one will blame you—you're simply saving your ass. But it's worth remembering that the ass you save may be subjected to actions by members of their Probe-itarian Club. And you may be forced to wear silver lamé boots.

☐ Minot? Why not?!!

☐ Rumor has it that the aliens are huge Dallas Cowboys fans, and this explains the twenty-story star decals on their ships. They apparently can't wait to meet (and maybe eat) Jerry Jones. See if the Cowboys' organization is currently hiring. Start wearing Cowboys-themed gear *now*.

☐ Watch for Spielberg's reaction. It should be priceless!

☐ Nothing matters now. Eat every donut you want. Order double pepperoni with stuffed-crust pizzas. Get a donut pizza for all we care.

☐ Again, if you're part of the Resistance, try to exclusively operate in urban areas. A resistance of two in Smallberg won't be productive.

☐ Watch for Tom Cruise's reaction when he realizes these aliens aren't related to Xenu. It should be hilarious!

☐ Make yourself as unappetizing as possible. Toughen your skin. Use makeup to give yourself fake wounds. Look as disheveled as a beat poet on a bender.

Interdimensional, Pastel-Colored, Man-Eating Ponies!

The Grim Rating:

Not exactly Secretariat—1.5.

"One of my visions: the Petting Zoo of Pain. A place where Mom, Dad, and the kids can go and get bitten by seemingly sweet creatures. These cutesy pony critters might be a fine place to start."

How It'll Go Down: It'll probably be the fault of that goofy Collider again (see next entry). A dimensional tear (which resembles a celestial hernia and can hurt like a sumbitch) will open in the Alps and thousands of the most appealing little ponies you'd ever want to see will stream into our plane of existence. There'll be every shade of pastel colors presented—precious pinks, lovely lavenders, soft greens, and dusty yellows. As scientists first observe the ponies, they'll seem docile

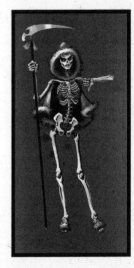

and harmless, grazing quietly and shimmering in the sun. The situation will take a nosedive when one of the scientists attempts to feed a carrot to a pony and loses an arm. Once the ponies taste flesh, they'll turn their pleasant pastel backs on the pastures of the past.

Thus, the reign of pony terror will begin. The Swiss Army will find that their nifty knives have no more effect on the evil equines than bullets. And the adorable devils will reproduce at an uncanny rate, giving birth to litters at a time. The ponies will spread from Europe into Asia and Africa, devouring sugar cubes and locals at will.

Estimated Length of Disaster: The man-eating ponies *can* stave off the damage from regular bullets, but it's soon discovered that higher caliber shells will take them out. The whole mess lasts less than four months. The hardest part will be stitching that dimensional tear back together.

Percentage of Population Affected: Maybe 2 or 3%.

A Shetland-sized list:

MAN-EATING PONIES BUCKET LIST

☐ Soak your sugar cubes in cyanide and coat your carrots with rat poison.

☐ Don't be fooled by how charming the ponies are. Their manes may flow like rainbows, but their teeth are razor-sharp. And don't put a saddle on one—they can't be domesticated.

☐ *Never* meet their dewy-eyed gaze. Those saucer eyes of theirs will suck you in.

☐ Hey, rodeo guy, did you *not* hear the part about domestication? Way to lasso one and lose a leg!

☐ And—we got nothin' else. Bring over your M61 Vulcan and help us get this wrapped up ASAP!

Part 4

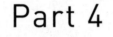

The Man-Made:
Handmade Hell

Large Hadron Collider Opens a Black Hole!

The Grim Rating:

Another 10?! You're too kind!

"Some of my best friends are black holes. I shit you not!"

How It'll Go Down: In June of 2016, a little-known Pakistani physicist will figure out a way to throw the Collider into "sixth gear" in order to increase the velocity of subatomic particles to such a degree they become nauseous. Once this experiment is performed and the acceleration takes place, the particles *will* get sick and spew gobs of quark-gluon plasma, a substance that sounds a lot neater than it is. This stuff looks, feels, and smells like curdled fish sauce. No thanks.

Anyway, this glop will gather itself into a puddle and burn an opening through our plane of existence, creating a small black hole beneath

Switzerland. As the hole expands, the circumstances will worsen and that's going to suck for everyone involved with the nearby 109th Annual Alps Yodelpalooza Convention and Concert at Montreux.

So much for neutrality—Switzerland gets first dibs at being sucked into the hole, followed by the rest of Europe and finally all of Earth. Not quite satisfied, the hole will search elsewhere for a digestif.

Estimated Length of Disaster: Six to seven days. This black hole is going to suffer from suction performance anxiety.

Percentage of Population Affected: Jeepers, everyone.

Your "hole" list:

BLACK HOLE BUCKET LIST

☐ Rent that time machine from your "associate" and figure out a subtle way to rub out the Pakistani guy while he's still young. Save the future while you can!

☐ (A) Get job at Collider—be willing to start in the kitchen if necessary, (B) locate which giant electrical outlet the Collider is plugged into, and (C) trip over the cord.

☐ Certain members of the scientific community have speculated that such a low-grade hole may be pluggable. Is Ron Jeremy available?

☐ While you're back in time icing the Pakistani, sabotage the construction of the Collider too. And make sure you wear camouflage. You know what they say: you can't spell "sabotage" without "camouflage!"

☐ If, as scientists claim, the quark-gluon plasma is actually a sentient being, see if it can be convinced into not becoming a black hole. Let it know it wasn't born a hole and has a choice to not be a hole. It can still be saved.

□ Feed tiny Tums to queasy protons.

□ Launch your children into space in hopes they land on a distant planet and become superheroes. You *have* been working on that rocket ship, right?

□ If you make it through the hole alive (which is—and we don't mean to be a bummer here—statistically improbable), please know that everything will look a lot different and you may resemble a blood-soaked Pixy Stick.

□ When the hole reaches your neighborhood, strap yourself into a lawn chair with a parachute attached. That should provide for one sweet ride!

Global Warming!

The Grim Rating:

Yesssss—9.2!

"I love long, luxurious disasters; they're like bubble baths. They don't create the logjams that a meteor or other forms of instantaneous snuff-dom do. Far better for me and, in the end, isn't that what it's all about?"

How It'll Go Down: Sooner than we'd like to think, the massive ice structures of the Arctic Ice Cap will, within the span of one week, break apart, as if they were being subjected to Mother Nature's Slap Chop. This will trigger a series of events to which Ticketmaster will attempt to insert itself. (A service charge for a *tsunami*? We think not.) We're talkin' fires, floods, and heaps of helmet-haired televangelists spewing vindictive things and providing no solace whatsoever.

We will be told by scientists that this is precisely what was predicted and that the days of worrying about our collective carbon footprint have passed. The tipping point has come and gone, and it's all downhill from here. This will be bad news for Prius sales and other green products. In typical fashion, the planet's populace will go to the extreme, consuming as many resources as are available before we run out of everything. Humans—we sorta suck.

Estimated Length of Disaster: From the ice cap breaking apart to the planet getting totally trashed—several months. These months will definitely make history's highlight reel.

Percentage of Population Affected: We won't lie to you—this is a biggee. At least 94% of all life could be exterminated by the multiple eco-dominos falling. It'll take a few years for the full impact to be felt, but this humdinger will be worth the wait.

The "Is anyone else in here warm?" list:

GLOBAL WARMING BUCKET LIST

☐ Don't buy bagged ice—there'll be plenty to go around.

☐ If you like disasters, this one will be grand. Every style and flavor of catastrophe will be featured. Look for this to be an Armageddon wonderland!

☐ Once the ice cap disintegrates, stop taking cruises. With the tidal waves and the free-range glaciers, such excursions will become little more than miserable thrill rides. Sorry, Royal Caribbean; I'd hoped we'd meet again— that chocolate fountain was sheer magic.

☐ Building a boat like Kon-Tiki might make for a fun family project!

☐ Start watching the SyFy channel. Its films offer loads of insight into how to cope with numerous environmental disasters. In our opinion, SyFy provides more answers than those dippy Discovery Channel shows. A series devoted to moonshiners? Uh-huh. That's educating us *how?*

☐ Wetlands *will* be wetter. Seek higher ground, grasshopper.

If you're in America, avoid Oklahoma. Between the rains, tornadoes, earthquakes, prairie fires, lava floes, oil spills, and noodlers injured by carp, it'll be dicey!

☐ All great natural disasters need a theme song. Get writin'!

☐ One of the beneficial effects of the cataclysm will be the new San Diego–like climate for Canada's Northwest Territories. Snap up those tundra tracts while prices are still low. We particularly like the Blubber Ridge development in the suburbs of Aklavik.

The Grim Rating:

Good things come in small packages—8.4!

"This whole age of nanotech is fascinating to me. Y'all believe these breakthroughs will enhance and extend your lives. Me, I *know* they'll go wrong and I'll end up making my quotas like always."

How It'll Go Down: Somewhere in the not-too-distant future, a prominent doctor will perform the first micro-micro surgery on a woman combating cancer. Dr. N. Tufnel, lead surgeon at the esteemed Liverpool Medical Center, will guide thousands of nanob search for malignant cells inside the patient. Each ti discover one, the mini-Roombas will hoover u repeating this procedure until all signs of ca

The surgery will be an unqualified success, except for when the diminutive droids finish, they'll refuse the exit command. Instead, they'll stream into the next available body, one of the assisting nurses. Once there, they'll inexplicably begin attacking every cell they can get their eensy-weensy mitts on. Within minutes, the poor nurse will become an iron-deficient husk.

As the bots interpret the data received from the first two procedures, they'll determine they did a bang-up job and gold stars will be awarded. They'll decide that, in order to do what's needed, they'll need to replicate themselves. Too bad the engineers who created the tiny automatons never devised a proper kill switch. No, they were too busy asking their iPhones moronic questions like "Have you seen my socks?"

Estimated Length of Disaster: Once the mechanotykes get their replication act together, they'll reach every continent within four years.

Percentage of Population Affected: About 82%. Again, the more remote your location is, the better off you'll be. And being surrounded by miles of water will be a plus.

Here's a little list:

NANOTECH BUCKET LIST

☐ Two cool ways to make yourself less drainable: (1) Triple your consumption of fish oil because the gooey gel messes with the bots' micro-treads; and (2) fill your home with ventriloquist dummies—these confuse the heck out of bots.

☐ It's theorized that, yet again, the colder regions will fare better. Decide now whether you'll want quality of life or quantity of life. This is not to say that one can't have a fine standard of living in subzero temps, but certainly arctic golfing is less appealing.

☐ Ask Japan to make miniature sex robots to alter the mission of the nanobots. A romantic distraction could mean the attack could be limited and they'd all hook up and settle down inside a rotund ex-Rugby player from Manchester. We believe that if anyone can figure out how to put miniscule dabs of lipstick on full little artificial mouths, the Japanese can!

☐ Do not use the Pore No Mo line of skin sealants.

- ☐ Increase your sodium intake exponentially. We don't know a single machine that enjoys salt.

- ☐ See to it that you and your battle team (include any Brazilian you can get named Gracie) are shrunk down to a microscopic size, injected into an infected body, and bust nano-butt!

- ☐ When the bot swarm comes under your door (it'll resemble a fine gray mist seeping into your home), drop an anvil on it. The Acme way *is* the best way.

- ☐ If you walk into a store and everyone looks like deflated lawn snow globes, say nothing and sneak away.

- ☐ Find out if Gort is willing to act as a mediator.

THE Killer Virus!

The Grim Rating:

A four-bagger! 9.3!!

"That's what I'm talkin' about—pestilence, suffering, and a lengthy time-line! Now, what can I do to those Cabal weenies?"

How It'll Go Down: In 2019, at an archaeological dig on the banks of the Tigris River, the ruins of an ancient town are uncovered. Upon further exploration, one of the structures is theorized to be a prehistoric pharmacy, complete with crusty vials and jars.

A worker hopped up on espresso drops and breaks an ancient vial while attempting to put it in a preservation container. He knows if he reveals what he did, he'll get written up again and that'll go in his personnel file. (Last quarter alone, he was responsible for three other viruses being released.) And so he says nothing and becomes the first carrier.

The virus will spread quicker than Snooki's legs once did, through the diggers and townsfolk, causing coughing, acute muscle spasms, and whining.

Because of the virus's age and complexity, an antidote won't be found until hundreds of millions of humans have died—and then there will barely be enough people left to make the necessary quantity of doses. Oh, and the rushed antidote will have one unfortunate side effect: every survivor will sound just like James Carville.

Interesting fact: 89% of all inoculations given out will go to rich white people, otherwise known as The Cabal (which is composed of .01% of the world's richest people). Through their influence, they'll manage to bypass the Powerball-like antidote lottery show entirely (and miss the opportunity to meet CNN's anchor/bombshell Erin Burnett). The Cabal's inoculations will be delivered directly to them—next-day air, even.

Estimated Length of Disaster: Within ten months, the virus will go global.

Percentage of Population Affected: About 93.5%. Ruh-roh.

This list is *sick*:

KILLER VIRUS BUCKET LIST

☐ If you're part of the Cabal, don't sweat it. "They've" got your back. (However, do be aware of this: it will only be a matter of time before the richest of the rich will need "help" again. You know, housework, nannies, mistresses. As a result, the richest *will* be looking to hire those who are slightly less rich for valuable opportunities. You rich folks are going to have to work that out amongst yourselves.)

☐ Everyone who isn't rich and white might want to keep a bottle of bleach handy. And antibacterial hand wash. And a gas mask. Oh, and don't forget gloves. Lots and lots of gloves.

☐ Limit exposure to fellow humans. Use Skype whenever possible.

☐ Have groceries delivered by a person in a Hazmat suit. Do not engage with him/her in any manner whatsoever. If said person attempts to ask a question, no matter how seemingly innocent, like "Can you *please* help me? I'm having trouble breathing!" say nothing and reseal door.

☐ Until it's determined whether the virus is airborne, cut back on frivolous breaths.

☐ Again, avoid watching any of the twenty-four-hour news stations—they'll have coo-ties. Instead, consider the recently launched YouFlu, the network with the most exclusive contagion content and a prime-time lineup of all flu-based entertainment. We think you'll love "Gramps Has the Cramps." Tuesdays at 9!

☐ Get your bunker together. It's time to upgrade your air filtration system with a higher quality model. And those shoddy re-placement filters you've been picking up at Ralph's don't cut it. Get real.

☐ If you choose to stay in the stock market, put together a pharmacentric portfolio because those companies will be peaking like fans at a Widespread Panic concert. Upside: with fewer people living, trades will go through more quickly!

☐ Once you and yours are "bunkerized," should any one of you become infected, immediately hold a family tribal council and vote the infected member out of the bunker.

☐ Give in to your OCD cleaning disorder. Indulge it daily.

Duggars!

The Grim Rating:

More for me—8.0!

"Folks who consistently overstock the population pond? Yes, please! They're filling my pantry. I'm definitely pro-Duggar—keep pluggin' away, Jim Bob!"

How It'll Go Down: It's estimated that in forty years, one out of every five people on our planet will be related to the endlessly spawning Duggar family of reality TV fame. Gross.

The reason why this is a *truly* insidious invasion is because of how far-reaching the Duggar gene pool will extend. No matter where you go in the future, there'll be a strong likelihood that someone you recently met, are dating, have slept with, work for, hired, or used to know is Duggar kin. What's that word? Oh yeah, *gross*.

Remember: Their mating habits were enhanced when biotech

advances enabled them to keep breeding into their sixties. With thirty-three in their original pack, it doesn't take a math whiz to see the potential for exponential damage. For example, while the little-woman-who-could was having her final young 'un, her first few spawn were already having *grandkids* of their own. Like a junkyard full of unneutered dogs, the crowd produced by this fanatically fertile family may outlast the resources available.

Estimated Length of Disaster: If their reproduction continues unabated, there'll be no stopping their attempt at the genetic conquest of Earth.

Percentage of Population Affected: It'll start at 20%, but move hastily upward as their rabbit-like breeding snowballs into the latter parts of the twenty-first century.

Check back in nine months—this list will have multiplied several times:

DUGGARS BUCKET LIST

☐ Begin a campaign to protect the future. Have a birth control gift basket delivered to their home with a handsome array of sponges, condoms, IUDs, Yaz, and anything else that could stop these über-birthers.

☐ If you can find a moment when they're not humping each other, see if the Chinese Minister of Procreation will pay Ma and Pa a visit. Will they listen to reason? If *China's* complaining about your incessant procreation, you might have a problem.

☐ Ask if you can have the pick of the litter.

☐ Sneak into their home at night and put salt-peter in everything they consume.

☐ Do your best to sabotage all biotech reproductive breakthroughs and/or severely limit the Duggars' access to such info. Bribe the hell out of their primary care physician.

☐ Pray to God for intervention. See if He's willing to personally visit them and say "Enough already!" Skeeter's all-in on this!

☐ Trick the Mrs. into taking a vacation twice a year—without her hubby. That should reduce the annual output by at least one.

☐ Plead with Arkansas legislators to create a "Baby Hoarding" statute limiting the number of toddlers one family can house.

☐ Have Mrs. Duggar's she-tunnel declared a historical landmark and not allow any more "renovation" to take place.

☐ Tell Paul Anka to shut the hell up.

The Grim Rating:

The glass is half-empty at 6.8.
"Should be higher, but what's a specter to do? Some folks don't eat. Bastards."

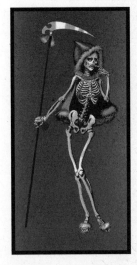

How It'll Go Down: This dreary disaster begins the day the last bee dies. The bee population will have become disillusioned with their perpetual pollination missions and, instead, will prefer to stay in its hives kicking back in mini-Barcaloungers. This bee-havior will lead to o-bee-sity, their eventual demise, and bee attributed to an unnamed company tinkering with plant DNA. Guess those nosy science nerds never considered the long-term consequences of their actions. Bio-douches.

Whatever the cause, the bees will perish and move on to the better hive of heaven. Oh, hell with it—thanks, Monsanto!

Without bees, a chain of events will be triggered—plants die, then animals, and then bingo, there's nothing to eat except each other. Donner, party of five?

Estimated Length of Disaster: Once the bees expire, it'll take four years for the ecosystem to cave in. When that happens, it ain't gonna be pretty.

Percentage of Population Affected: Anyone who has a need to nosh. Supermodels will be unaffected.

A meager list:

FAMINE BUCKET LIST

☐ Join Weight Watchers today! Take their point system and cut it in half. And then do that again.

☐ So the diet idea doesn't work for you? Then prior to the upcoming famine-fest, bulk up. Eat everything within arm's reach and gain as much weight as possible. Go full chub. With that kind of girth, there's a distinct chance that the famine will take one look at you and say, "No way I'm gonna work that hard!" On the other hand, your newfound flab may make you more attractive to the cannibalism cults. Choose your poison, bruh.

☐ When anarchy breaks out, put on your silk robe, the comfiest of slippers, and make yourself a strong Manhattan. What the hell—throw in an extra cherry. Life's shorter than ever!

☐ Get hip to what's considered the latest take on lovely—distended stomachs can be sexy! As they say, beauty's in the belly of the beholder.

- [ ] Cancel your subscriptions to *Bon Appétit* and *Gourmet*, and subscribe to *Cooking Really Really Really Light*.

- [ ] If you're reading this in the future and the collapse has begun, consider meeting your (and other's) culinary needs with a pica-esque approach. Wood, dirt, and such can be damn tasty, especially with Mrs. Butterworth's as a dipping sauce.

- [ ] Speaking of pica, here's a business idea: Open Pica's Place—an eating disorder-themed bar/restaurant. Offer a Penny Colada—and a Toilet Paper Panini.

- [ ] Stop using your catchphrase, "Stay hungry, my friends." No one's laughing at it.

- [ ] If you chose to gain a lot of weight and the cannibals notice you, let your personal hygiene go to hell. One idea: buy one of those hairbrained Forever Lazy blanket-suits and repeatedly soil yourself. That's a start.

Feast!

The Grim Rating:

Decent enough, I suppose—7.1.

"It's an unenthused 7.1, *okay*?? But here's a sweet story: Whenever I'm required to remove a large person from your reality, I think back on something my dad told me. He looked at me one day and said, 'Hon, by taking out the big one, it'll make room for two or three of the smaller ones.' He had a special way of seeing things."

How It'll Go Down: In the twenty-second century, every disease will be cured. The human lifespan will increase at an unheard-of rate due to transplants, bionics, and the sensational home organ-growing kits from Mr. Liver, the first name in DIY personal-tissue production. Additionally, genetically altered crops and livestock will provide more than enough for everyone to eat well, *extremely* well.

This seemingly perfect era for mankind will have one downside: global obesity. There will be such an abundance of food for everyone that the world's population will become plump. Even Kenyans, who won't even be able to finish marathons anymore.

There will be speculation within the scientific community that something within the lab-created food makes it addictive. This theory will hold water, every bit as much as the human race's bloated bodies.

Estimated Length of Disaster: A couple of decades in and folks will begin to spontaneously croak and fall over. This will make for precarious (and embarrassing) situations whereby innocent folks will get squished by the podgy falling bodies. Also, most ambulances (and hearses) will have to be retrofitted with heavy-duty shocks and heftier tires in order to the tote the bulging bods.

Percentage of Population Affected: Close to 84%.

I couldn't *think* of eating another list:

FEAST BUCKET LIST

☐ Find a few packets of heirloom seeds and plant a veggie garden. Once that's growing, don't eat anything, anytime, anywhere from any place other than your garden or livestock supply (if you choose to go that route). All it takes is three of the faux food meals and you're hooked. Hooked, I tell you!

☐ As for you folks who don't care about getting addicted to the lab chow, eat up. Your life just became Möbius strip at the Golden Corral.

☐ The bio-vittles are not without their moments. Whoever thought of infusing pig DNA with maple flavoring is nothing short of a genius. Bravo!

☐ Two powerful words for the comeback pants of tomorrow: Sansa Belts.

☐ As you head toward that massive heart attack, remember how comfy a muumuu can be. Go ahead and call it a caftan if that makes you feel better.

☐ In addition to the weight gain, you'll experience noticeable hormonal changes. Gals, you may have to start shaving—your faces, that is. Guys, you'll love having breasts but won't enjoy the frequent crying jags. Or getting your bras on and off—it's a whole different deal when *you're* wearing 'em.

☐ Put your Vespa in storage—it's no longer an option.

☐ If you end up addicted, help is available at the New Olde World Country Buffet Recovery Center. Their remarkable program will end the chicken-fried cravings and mac and cheese attacks. You don't have to live like that—there's a better way at the New Olde World Country Buffet.

A Bad Case of Zombie Outbreak!

The Grim Rating:

What a bunch of stiffs—4.6.

"Why can't the dead stay dead? I don't ask for much."

How It'll Go Down: This is *not* an invasion—fooled ya! This one has "man-made" written all over its decomposing face.

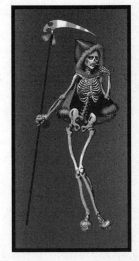

As has been documented in several books, a cadre of corporate scientists will test a deadly virus by secretly unleashing it upon part of a pizza-ordering neighborhood near their lab. Not surprisingly, when their plan tanks and the antidote fails, the virus spreads, zombifying the victims within hours. That's what the pizza-consuming public gets for ordering pineapple on their pies. Yeesh!

Some of the infected will have their symptoms minimized by a helpful program designed for the recently bitten. This will involve a regimen of drugs, exercise, and economic consumption. It's *because* of this intrepid program that the virus is eventually stopped in its tracks and the zombies are contained and eventually given their own tiny country. Not long afterward, life returns to normal. Mostly.

Estimated Length of Disaster: Several years. During this time, there'll be a crapload of very enthused zombie fans taking this in. This will be everything they've ever dreamed of!

Percentage of Population Affected: Maybe 31% all told. We've seen worse. (Ironically, author Max Brooks is killed by a zombie within the first two days.)

Bring out your list:

ZOMBIES BUCKET LIST

☐ Don't get bit and don't order any delivery pizza. C'mon, using pizza as part of a scientific experiment? Is nothing sacred??

☐ It's a known fact that a trowel, when thrust into a zombie's forehead, will produce fine results. We find that trowelandtrue.com offers a superior assortment of tools.

☐ We understand that if you're bitten, a drug called Romerin will help you feel better. Isn't *that* good to know?

☐ Knowledge is the best weapon, so learn as much as you can about your enemy. Consider getting your PhZ.

☐ You may start seeing a 30-minute infomercial called "The Shores of Your Future," concocted by and starring a quack named Dr. Kenneth Beaker. He'll be trying to sell you on the idea of moving into one of his weird assisted post-living facilities—if you're infected, that is. Turn that shit off.

☐ If you spot an actual flesh head, call the Paraguard and wait for their bright orange trucks to arrive. Let the professionals take care of the shambling fool.

☐ Stay away from zombie walks—there are genuine zombies out there and they're trying to blend in! Their strategy: Bite in plain sight.

☐ A Containment Zone is *not* a tourist attraction. We don't care if there is a dynamite gift shop—steer clear of these fortresses. They're full of *zombies*, ya dope!

☐ Don't spend time in graveyards or in trucks on fire.

☐ Try not to get caught being the only African American in a white Southern county overrun by zombies. Accidents happen.

Genetically Altered Food!

The Grim Rating:

So close and yet—9.4.

"Holy cow, this one's gonna drag its altered ass around for a while. I must admit, though, the mutations will be a gas to watch!"

How It'll Go Down: This food is responsible for quite a few disasters in this book. We figured it was time for it to be properly highlighted.

By the year 2027, 92.4% of all things eaten will be either genetically altered or synthetic. From corn to wheat to livestock, nearly everything will have had its DNA screwed with. At first this will cause no problems—the world needed the food. Frankly, the genetic stuff will frequently taste better than the original: grains grainier, pork porkier, and so and so on-ier. We don't know how they do it! Well, we *do* know but would rather not think about it.

It'll take a full ten years of ingesting this crud before mutations begin to manifest—an extra limb here, a set of gills there. Sadly, these mutations won't only happen to newborns—they'll also occur in adults. And your tail won't magically appear in a day; no, it'll slowly and painfully begin to protrude from your coccyx and hurt like hell.

Many people won't survive the mutations. This will lead to two classes of people left populating the planet: those with genetic deformities and a few million "normal" folks who never bought into the altered grub and continued to shop at pricey health food stores. (Yes, Whole Foods, your future looks bright.)

Estimated Length of Disaster: Fifteen to twenty years.

Percentage of Population Affected: 98.2%. Eek.

Here's your list, muties:

ALTERED FOOD BUCKET LIST

☐ Obviously, if you want to be part of the 1.8% who survive and still appear normal, start ponying up the mega-kwan for items such as Tofurkey and Soylami. Might we recommend our store, Uncle Hank's Health Hut. Our prices are competitive and we guarantee our employees don't have gills. Yet.

☐ Sneak into experimental cornfields and sing a verse or two of "Just the Way You Are."

☐ The engineered bacon is so sublime, it's capable of producing a sensory experience that can cause spontaneous orgasms in men and women alike. Keep that in mind when breakfasting in public.

☐ If you start to sprout a prehensile tail, don't panic. As it emerges, learn to love it as you would any other body part. Get a tail cozy and wear it proudly.

☐ With the right kind of shirt or blouse collar, gills can be bangin'. Eschew the turtleneck and go for the Mandarin or Wing instead. Let your freak flag fly!

☐ Assuming your given mutation doesn't kill you, don't let your self-esteem slide during this time. Your "enhancements" might be just what you've always needed. Who among us hasn't said at one time or another, "I could sure use an extra hand?"

☐ Find out exactly what mutations are covered by your current health insurance provider. Is fifth nipple excluded?

☐ Whatever you do, don't end up like that Kuato dude in *Total Recall.* That homie was pure puppet show from the neck down!

HAARP!

The Grim Rating:

Let the good times roll—9.3!

"There's nothing better in this deathtime than when man starts monkeying around with stuff he has no business playing with. It always produces endless laughs—and results—for me."

How It'll Go Down: Contrary to popular belief, HAARP is *not* a blues harmonica society for senior citizens. No, HAARP stands for the High-Frequency Active Auroral Research Program, which does nothing to explain what it actually is. Here's what they want you to believe: HAARP is a perfectly innocent project in Alaska that's part of the Strategic Defense Initiative. Here's what the truth is: HAARP is more like a weapon/device from the demented mind of a James Bond villain.

Several years from now, researchers will be performing a routine

multibajillion megawatt blast into the ionosphere that produces an effect a lot like slipping it a Cialis. During the procedure, the lead scientist's aorta will rupture from an unaddressed aneurysm and he'll die. By the time the rest of the research team realizes something's gone wrong, the blast will have gone on three times longer than it should've, and the damage will be done. Because of this prolonged jolt, the wood that the ionosphere will be sporting will require it to unleash powerful and erratic weather patterns the likes of which have only been witnessed by Helen Hunt in *Twister*.

Estimated Length of Disaster: This bastard is one for the ages. Every kind of meteorological catastrophe will be featured here, and these vibrant systems will sure take their sweet time dissipating. During Weather Channel remote broadcasts, the excitement level will be so palpable that, at the end of week two, Jim Cantore will literally explode on the air. Great for ratings—bad for him.

Percentage of Population Affected: This time the arctic regions get firsties as the atmospheric storms will spread to the south. Nature has a chance to hang a hundred on us—percentage points that is!

Your list on the eights:

HAARP BUCKET LIST

☐ Go back to 1993 and convince the military that you can do a better job building the facility than some company named BAE Advanced Technologies. (Like *it* knows what it's doing!) Anyway, once you snag the contract, build the device out of papier mâché.

☐ Seek to expose that S'tan is the individual behind HAARP. Take photos of him at the facility. Get a close-up of his pointy tail. Sell the pics to TMZ.

☐ While hang gliding into the facility (wearing your best stealth cloak), throw a dime into the mechanism. These science guys we know believe a single coin can short-circuit the device *and* bring down the grid. And when you throw that dime in, don't forget to make a wish! World peace?

☐ Open a storm-chasing/tourism business and take out a hefty insurance policy.

☐ Use a "whole-house" C-clamp to secure your roof.

☐ In a well-choreographed cinematic moment, have multiple helicopters ready to take you and your loved ones to a safer locale. If at all possible, wait until dusk when the light is warm and sugary. Then—let the choppers fly!

☐ Dig a moat as deep as you can around your abode. This may help stem the flow of water, mud, magma, bodies, debris, rocks, bodies, trees, cars, bodies, and sewage.

☐ Next time you catch wind that an oversized Japanese monster is looking for distinctive potential targets, suggest HAARP.

☐ Tell the ionosphere to get its rocks off elsewhere.

Chemtrails!

The Grim Rating:

It's a jump Ca-ball—4.1.

"I like to think I'm open-minded, but the ass faces from the Cabal irk me. Normally, I appreciate help, but *these* folks—wow! It *must* be bad when the Specter of Death thinks you're scum."

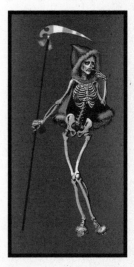

How It'll Go Down: For several decades now, military airplanes have been dousing us with toxins from extremely high altitudes. Why? Because our planet was never meant to sustain this many people. So, forty years ago, a plan was put into motion by The Cabal to cull the herd before the herd got out of control.

Truth be told, the herd got bigger far too quickly—The Cabal underestimated us. With longevity increasing and not nearly enough plagues and catastrophes to help the cause, it will become necessary for The

Cabal to kick its campaign into a higher gear. This means we'll be seeing more flights over major cities, creating a latticework of trails resembling the Tholian Web. (You Trekkies know what a bitch that can be!) These flights will release even more lethal compounds meant to shorten our lives, make us sterile, and dull our minds. Think of it as crop dusting—only we're the crops *and* the bugs.

Interesting fact: The difference between a chemtrail and a regular airplane contrail is that chemtrails are much, much wider. A sign of having witnessed a chemtrail? An hour after noticing it, you've coughed up a kidney.

Estimated Length of Disaster: Word has it that The Cabal is extremely concerned about its members' quality of life in the coming years. Consequently, expect an aggressive drive to impede the spinning integers on the population tote board. The Cabal will start seeing positive results within the first two years of its increased efforts and be greatly pleased.

Percentage of Population Affected: As many as The Cabal can manage!

Hey, look—a skywriter is writing the word "list"!

CHEMTRAILS BUCKET LIST

☐ Cover your car with a tarp—those compounds can eff up your rims!

☐ A quaint picnic in your basement can be every bit as charming and far easier on your respiratory system.

☐ We're patriotic, but it's okay for you to *not* be down with what The Cabal's doing. Feel free to decline if asked to croak early because unnamed billionaires and their families need your oxygen. You've got rights too—even if they don't count as much.

☐ If you get coated in chemicals, keep in mind that it will take more than one dose to frag you. (Best estimates indicate three to five dousings will cause you irreparable damage.) Get into the shower immediately. And don't bother with the loofah—reach for that steel wool and dig in!

☐ Anger is not a particularly productive emotion unless you're an action hero on a vendetta against mob members who killed your sleeping relatives. Try to understand that The

Cabal wants to offer its members' descendants better lives and is willing to sacrifice yours to make that happen. It's kinda touching when you think about it.

☐ You'd be surprised to learn that it's not just *your* government that's participating in the chemtrails—this is an international effort. Greed knows no boundaries. It's comforting to realize that we, as a people, can come together for the big stuff.

☐ We've said it before, we'll say it again: Never take lightly the efficacy of a high-quality Hazmat suit. Don't settle for inferior brands such as the "Haz-Mate" or the "Hazmat Snuggie." Fleece serves no purpose here.

☐ You can aim your laser pointer at the planes, but it's doubtful you'll hit one. They're waaay up there and you're waaay down here. And, as you may have guessed, they're moving at quite a clip. A black market rocket launcher won't work either—they're rarely dependable. But FYI, once you attempt to use that laser, The Cabal will have your coordinates. You don't want that.

☐ Speaking of The Cabal, the friendly folks behind the chemtrails would appreciate it if you'd consider their "buyout" offers arriving in the mail soon. By accepting an offer, much time and effort will be saved and your family will be handsomely rewarded for your absence. Simply sign the form and they'll take care of the rest. Your family will start getting those checks within the week!

☐ No need to sign an organ donor card now. Other than The Cabal, no one's getting a new anything.

Dimensional Shift Causes Complete Collapse of Space-Time Continuum!

The Grim Rating:

Uhhhhhh—4.3 to 11. (Possible bonus for extra dimensions.)

"I'll remain unconvinced until the final tally. But truly, I hate cosmic crap that involves uncertainties beyond my control. It makes planning ahead a bitch!"

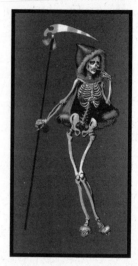

How It'll Go Down: Gosh, this one sounds awful.

Apparently, several years from now, a few eggheads in China will be dickin' around with their latest invention: lab-created neutrinos. When the feisty particles are introduced to the more retiring common neutrinos, sparks will fly and the two types will start dry humping each other on a subatomic level.

This micromating will cause a momentary blink of darkness followed by several gruesome moments where reality will appear to be cubist. To be more accurate, probably closer to Russian neo-primitivist, but what the hell. Either way, it's gonna hurt.

As this disaster progresses, the cumulative strata of the multiverse will merge and disintegrate. This traditionally leads to nosebleeds and nonexistence. Bottom line: reality will flicker and collapse, and you won't make it to the club that night to see that Nickelback cover band you like.

Estimated Length of Disaster: From the time the neutrinos hook-up until they trigger the epic crash of existence—not sure, but it'll probably be same-day service.

Percentage of Population Affected: Maybe everyone, everywhere, everywhen. But who knows, really? No one has experienced this before—it's a crapshoot.

Our best guess at a list (which still makes for a better reality than that of a Nickelback cover band):

DIMENSIONAL COLLAPSE BUCKET LIST

☐ In case you miraculously survive, make the best of any additional appendages you may gain in the primordial merging. A fin could come in handier than you would have ever believed!

☐ Study *Guernica* to get a rough feel for how reality will look.

☐ Friend Brian Greene on Facebook, like, now.

☐ Watch that classic *Trek* episode where there's an evil version of the Enterprise and the good Kirk has that hot "Captain's Woman" and the bad Spock has that bitchin' Van Dyke and he ends up helping the good Kirk. That'll help you understand your future. Or not. Anyway, it's an awesome episode and who knows—you could soon meet your Bizarro self.

☐ Some people will see portals open during the collapse. The images inside will be glimpses of different dimensional locales, such as the swaying mercury windmills of Zhandoo or the fourteenth tee at the Bruntosan Country Club and Slaughterhouse. If you're lucky enough to see a portal and it shows you a picture of a swell setting, for Pete's sake, jump!

☐ Buy a box of earplugs. It's theorized that the end of existence makes a terrific racket!

☐ If you *are* exposed to a portal and decide to enter it, consider lubing up really well first (mineral oil, butter, what have you) to ease the pain associated with "interdimensional penetration."

☐ Prior to the cataclysm, take in as much science as you can, even if it's only on TV. Again, you'll need all your cognitive skills in order to survive the amount of sensory distortion that'll be coming your way. Avoid RFD-TV during this time. *Hee Haw* reruns sure won't save you.

☐ Or screw it—max out your credit cards and throw all fiscal caution to the wind. Like the collection agency is gonna track you down on Zhandoo? *Not.*

Ninjas!

The Grim Rating:

Flop like the wind—5.3.

"I'm eternally entertained by the human capacity to not know when to stop. You get a good thing happening and then you have to push it, even the alleged mystics. Hey, ninjas, wanna rumble? My scythe versus your swords. It's go time!"

How It'll Go Down: Following the Japanese economic meltdown of 2027, there'll be a backlash against the pitiable governmental and personal choices that placed the populace in such a precarious position. We'll see Japan go retro, and by retro, we mean the fifteenth century.

Ninjas will stage a comeback and make quite the splash in everyday Japanese life. The shadowy guys will appear everywhere—as car salesmen, bartenders, and TV talk show hosts. A youth organization

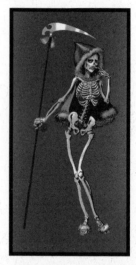

called Ninja Scouts will surface whose members will earn badges for activities like gutting and dematerializing.

Eventually, the ninjas will form the Shinobi Party, which will run unopposed in the 2030 elections, the other candidates having mysteriously dropped out. An anchorman who refers to himself as "the Wolf Blitzer of Tokyo" will confidently project the Shinobi as winners before the polls even open.

All of this will Japan to avoid a complete societal breakdown. The *real* problems will start when the Shinobi Party seeks to globally franchise itself to convert the world to the way of the warrior. And those Ninja Scouts will be *all* jacked-up about that idea.

Estimated Length of Disaster: China, which has its own history with ninjas, will take umbrage at Japan's approach and lead the fight against the Shinobi. Consequently, the Party's attempt at expansion will be crushed within six months. But know this: the fight scenes between the two clans will be Kurosawa crossed with Woo giving birth to Tsui Hark—all sorts of awesome!

Percentage of Population Affected: 8%, tops.

This list was never here. (What list?) Exactly.

NINJAS BUCKET LIST

☐ When Ninja Scouts knock on your door, don't move and don't answer.

☐ Find an alchemist who can make a potion that trasmutes Tamahagane steel into rubber. Watch ninjas' minds get blown when their swords bounce off!

☐ Create *NinjaMatch* dating site. Those phantoms could use a little relief.

☐ Wear a carbon-fiber-reinforced polymer vest at all times. When a ninja attempts to pull your heart out (because they *always* try to do that), his fist will get hurty.

☐ Explain to the attacking ninjas that you're comfortable with your life and life choices. You wish them well in their endeavors, but would they please leave your head attached to your neck?

☐ Wear a fake ninja suit and appear aloof and all-knowing. They'll never attack one of their own.

Mass Hysteria, Madness, and Mayhem!

The Grim Rating:

A paltry effort—2.8.

"After the amount of time I've spent in this plane of existence, I deserve better. That's all I've got to say."

How It'll Go Down: Anyone who's familiar with the human race's antics knows it doesn't take much to make us lose our cool. As a species, we're as spookable as they come, second only to the inhabitants of Glatni IV in the Ringbelt of Snor, who spend their entire existences cowering from imagined threats outside their caves. But it's a close second.

And so it will be that the combination of a severe flu season, an international meat recall, and a global economic crisis will cause millions of people to jump to the preposterous conclusion that *this* is the end of the world. Rumors will persist about how this flu is the same virus that's tainted the meat supply and that's why there's a global financial meltdown. Not surprisingly, mobs will form, burn cars, and do all manner of mobby stuff that mobby mobs do. Survivalists will then spring into action and implement every one of their inane plans. That's when things will *really* get juicy!

This, in fact, will *not* be the end of the world, but that won't stop our dignified brethren from torching buildings or shooting anyone who gets in their way at a Cabela's or other odd stores that feature babbling brooks and indoor pheasant hunting.

Estimated Length of Disaster: Most of the winter and into the spring. The flu season will pass, the bad meat will be disposed of (or made into taco filling), and international banks will forgive a shit ton of debt. Life will resume, at least for those who are left living.

Percentage of Population Affected: More than you'd like to believe.

Here's your list, ya maniacs:

MASS HYSTERIA BUCKET LIST

☐ If a wild-eyed guy wants to cut in front of you in the Target express checkout line, let him. And do the same for anyone else who seems to be breathing heavily or is unusually sweaty. These folks are on a mission you don't want to know about.

☐ Yes, it's a bad flu, but it's not THE killer virus. Likewise with the economic news and the tainted meat. Chug Nyquil, keep your savings in a dresser drawer, eat a veggie burger or three, and don't get murdered. Not that difficult.

☐ Stay away from Home Depot, Lowe's, and any similar stores. Those places are gonna be nut magnets.

☐ Martial law will be declared and strict curfews will be enforced, so don't end up in the hoosegow. Interesting fact: These curfews will cause a dating crisis in the singles world and for cheating spouses. Lunchtime hookups will become the new norm, which, with the increased urgency, can be hotter. Daytime motel rates will skyrocket.

☐ Social network sites will be overwhelmed with negativity and panic. Many Tweets will consist of nothing but gibberish, all caps, and exclamation points. DON'T GIVE IN TO THE *#$^&&& HYSTERIA!!!!!!

☐ Possible business venture: In the tradition of food trucks, offer riot supplies out of your van. Volume discounting on rocks and bottles!

☐ The good news is the Westboro Baptist Church will be spread paper-thin by having to protest at so many locations. Its effectiveness will be greatly reduced as its members also catch the flu. Their God must hate them. Skeeter sure does!

Nice Goin', Mankind—We're Talkin' Another Friggin' Ice Age!

The Grim Rating:

A stone-cold 8.7!

"Everyone thinks I'm a warm weather kind of gal—maybe it's my garb, I don't know. But I enjoy the winter, especially when it lasts a couple of centuries. And if it's any comfort, I *really* enjoy claiming weathermen. Forecast *that*, jerks!"

How It'll Go Down: Nothing natural about this one—we did it to ourselves. As for global warming, not so much. Turns out everybody got it wrong and instead, the truth was more about global cooling.

One year, spring never arrives in the Northern Hemisphere. Memorial Day rolls around and it's still snowing like the bejeezus over most of North America and southern Europe. Of course the weathermen are all like, "This continues to be an unusual front, but it should lift soon and blah blah blah," but it doesn't lift and they look like complete assholes as the weeks go by.

No one gets panicky until a blizzard hits Southern California. That's when the United States comes unglued and people are *pissed*. Six out of ten of the individuals on the FBI's most wanted list are weathermen. The situation turns for the worse when Willard Scott is attacked by a 100-year-old guy in a Smucker's sweatshirt during a remote segment in snowy Central Park.

Estimated Length of Disaster: It'll take about two years to completely ice up the joint.

Percentage of Population Affected: About 90%. Those creeps at the equator will be spared.

Chill with this list, my brothuh:

ICE AGE BUCKET LIST

☐ Time to purchase that swanky parka you've been admiring at your fave high-end camping store. Buy it a notch or two larger than what you normally wear because you'll be lining it with a down comforter and as many rolls of Owens Corning R-38 Insulation as you can pack in. You'll look bulky, but you'll be toasty!

☐ Get on the flat payment plan with your heating utility provider. That way, you won't have to immediately deal with the upcoming 1257% spike in your bill.

☐ You can officially stop trying to Save the Polar Bears. Those critters will finally get a needed break.

☐ Get as much firewood and/or as many freakin' Duraflames as you can. And if you don't have a fireplace, get that too.

☐ Find out where this mystifying "equator" is and research property prices in the area. Maybe a multi-decade rental while the glacial sheets recede?

☐ Consider a trip to Jukkasjärvi, Sweden, for a stay at its nutty ice hotel. That should (A) give you a feel for what's headed your way and (B) motivate the heck out of ya. But a piece of advice—don't use the ice bidet.

☐ Does anyone make orthopedic snowshoes?

☐ Disable your fridge's icemaker.

☐ Try not to wince when Al Gore rubs it in on Letterman.

WWIII!

The Grim Rating:

A glowing 8.8!

"Zombies *again*? When did they become overachievers? Oh well. At least, in this case, they're bringing me work."

How It'll Go Down: The living-dead nation of Zombistan gets what's left of its hands on a few of the former Soviet Union's atomic warheads. (They were on special at a flea market.) Apparently, the USSR had hoarding tendencies with missiles literally lying around the Kremlin, cluttering up the living room, and even had one stashed under a kid's bed. After the wife lowered the boom, the USSR was "encouraged" to clean up its mess and begrudgingly took the missiles to the aforementioned flea market. This is how the weaponry came to be sold to an unsavory deadish individual with a roll of fifties.

Once Zombistanian officials obtain the twenty-two WMDs, they'll hire a few smart people to aim the missiles at world capitals and let 'em fly. While the birds are in the air, the next phase of the assault happens—the Zombistanian Army shambles into nearby countries, bringing the bite to their enemies.

However, because they're zombies and not quite brilliant, the Zombistanians neglect to realize that the fallout from their warheads and the inevitable retaliatory strikes will do a number on our planet *and* its populace, making most folks too radioactive to be tasty.

Estimated Length of Disaster: As the fallout spreads, it will only be a matter of weeks before we're screwed. Effin' zombies! Always messing around with shit they don't understand, like malls or WMDs.

Percentage of Population Affected: About 90%. Due to geographic isolation, Australia dodges a big bullet here along with most people who live in rural areas, far away from cities. Unfortunately, this will mean that the remaining population on Earth will fall somewhere between *Crocodile Dundee* and *Deliverance*. Banjos and shrimp on the barbie, mate.

This list is downright radiant:

WWIII BUCKET LIST

☐ You've always dreamed of a trip to Australia. It's time to go!

☐ You *do* know that the whole "duck and cover" bit is complete rubbish, right? And that bunker we've referred to? Better make it comfy 'cause you'll be lodging there a while. Like, generations.

☐ Try to prevent the entire mess from happening. When the United Nations brings up a vote on statehood for zombies, protest the action. It's the dumbest idea ever. Palestinians *still* don't have a country, but zombies should? What the hell?

☐ If you live in Moscow, D.C., London, Tokyo, or any other high-profile capital cities, you may want to transition to a more simple, agrarian lifestyle. Somewhere quaint and remote.

☐ And you certainly don't want to "wait it out" and see what happens. You can't do that. The shockwave alone will flatten all of your stuff along with *you*, which means you won't have you or your stuff anymore. That'll suck. In other words, take action to be where the shock waves won't be. You understand that, right? So why are you still giving us that blank look?

☐ Hey, Californians, if you move to another state—a state less entangled in, shall we say, the entertainment industry—please keep in mind that no one will care about your latest screenplay. Or your supposed recurring role as the kindly professor on that pathetic TV Land show. Try this: Keep your yap shut and attempt to blend in.

☐ Another fine business move during this time—open a mortuary.

☐ Probably no opportunity for a snake purchase here, but you can try! See if Billy Jim has any specials goin'.

Jingle Sung by Hasselhoff Causes Heads to Explode!

The Grim Rating:

I don't even have a nose and mine bled—3.8.

"Effin' Hasselhoff. I thought I had him years ago with that classic drunken cheeseburger trick."

How It'll Go Down: Der Burger Haus, a fourth-rate German fast food franchise, will look to boost its business by moving into the U.S. market. The chain will hire an ad agency who will employ the supposedly in vogue hip-hop star/producer DJ Morty. The dubious DJ will write and produce a jingle for American radio, and in a head-scratching moment, he will hire David Hasselhoff to sing it.

When the radio spots are played for the Burger execs, a few noses bleed, but no one thinks much of that—it happens at corporate.

The next day, Morty will tweak the jingle by layering in more samples and additional instances of Mr. Hasselhoff singing "uh-huh." What Morty doesn't know is his jingle will become a lethal creation. Like the painting that ate Paris, a confluence of random elements has turned the original product into a deadly thing. Maybe it's the vocal delivery of this couplet—"an abundance of riches/with my all-beef bitches"—that pushed it over the edge. Who can say?

Once the ads begin to air, emergency calls will pour in—it seems people's heads, like Spinal Tap drummers, are exploding. Folks will be innocently listening to the commercial when suddenly they'll stiffen and gurgle, and within moments, their stiffen and gurgle, and within moments, their heads will swell and blow up. Good luck getting that out of the carpet!

Estimated Length of Disaster: It'll take about a month before the authorities can determine that the jingle is the culprit. By the time this is discerned, the ad will have gone viral over the Net and the carnage will be considerable.

Percentage of Population Affected: Maybe 17%. Let's face it, despite the hoopla and bloodshed, the commercial will still blow.

The list, yo:

LETHAL JINGLE BUCKET LIST

☐ For Skeeter's sake, if the ad comes on, don't watch it or hum along. Turn it off!

☐ And certainly don't go to the Der Der Burger Haus YouTube channel, even if they offer a downloadable coupon for a Haus Kid's BeatBox with the Hasselhoff action figure.

☐ While much can be pinned on Hasselhoff, this one is on Morty. Boycott his products, including his designer vodka, Bitchwheat, and his baking mix, Bitchquick.

☐ Pass new federal standards limiting the nature of samples that can be subliminally used in commercials. Certainly the inclusion of sizzling grill sounds, growling stomachs, and women's orgasms should be off the table.

☐ Here's another opportunity to rent the time machine from that guy. (But tell him this time you're *not* laying out all that cash as a deposit. No way.) Go back about five years and convince the slightly younger Morty that he is, in fact, every bit as lacking in talent as his parents always claimed.

☐ Find creative ways to use the jingle, for ex-ample: Place ear plugs in ears; transfer jingle onto ancient cassette format; place cassette in boom box; stand outside the home of Karl Rove, holding boom box above head like John Cusack; and press Play. No? Fine, then do the same thing, but at...we don't know—Harry Reid's house. This isn't a partisan issue.

☐ Morty needs to be prosecuted to the full-est extent of the law. But don't allow him to represent himself—he'll attempt to rap his defense. Unacceptable.

☐ And certainly do *not* buy Morty's spin-off CD—*The DJ Morty Platinum Joynt* featuring his latest song, "Fish Stick Bitches."

☐ We *told* you not to hum along. Now look what you've done to your head!

The Grim Rating:

How low can you go? 1.1.

"Despite the lousy score here, I must confess I'm a big fan of The Sack. I was pleased he and I were able to make a deal—I took his soul, he got some chops. Win, win—kind of."

How It'll Go Down: Ekonomy Karma, a psycho-delic (*its* spelling), big-hair band billing itself as "The Most Deafeningest" will, one evening in August 2015, perform its hit "Metallurgy Urges" at California's Riverside Amphibiantheater. During the tune, bassist Mack "The Nutsack" (usually shortened to "Sack") McIntyre will suffer a blood-clot brain freeze and be unable to stop his extended bass solo.

By minute eighteen, fans will stop waving lighters and start pleading for him to stop. By minute forty-two, the rest of the band will notice something's wrong. By minute sixty-three, the planet will get peeved and end his solo by tripping a major fault directly beneath the Amphibiantheater.

The 7.9 Riverside Quake will not only end his solo, but also the lives of the band and anyone else who was dense enough to stick around for a sixty-three-minute bass solo. Sadly, this quake will trigger several others, and, as a result, much of SoCal's beloved Inland Empire will be lost.

Estimated Length of Disaster: Those low frequencies get on Earth's last nerve, so it'll depend on how punishing Earth intends to be. If it's feeling charitable that day, it'll take out only the Inland Empire. If not, the tremors could last for months and a number of other faults could be nudged in nearby Arizona and Nevada.

Percentage of Population Affected: Hard to know. Probably less than 1%.

Pump up da list:

BASS SOLO BUCKET LIST

☐ If you're goin' to the concert, get a few hits of the latest designer brew your neighbor's been cookin'. That last batch definitely shaved your skull cap.

☐ Dude, save up the Benjamins and have "The Sack" tattooed on *your* sack. That'll impress the chicks.

☐ If you're at the event and the solo starts, excuse yourself politely and exit the Amphibiantheater in a hurried manner. You're on the clock!

☐ Get a pair of "Sack-Canceling" headphones from Bose.

☐ Now that you know how much Mother Earth despises extremely low frequencies, consider *not* putting that studio-grade sub-woofer into your tricked-out Eclipse. Our planet-spirit can generate a sinkhole in a New York minute. Keep that in mind.

☐ Pre-show: Sailor Jerry, Diet Dew, Tombstone pizzas, and three of those blue pills.

☐ Post-show: hookah, bath salts, Hennessy, Diet Coke, and a couple of games of Mineral Oil Twister. Hells yeah!

☐ If you're not going to the concert, would you mind checking in on my old lady, man? I think she got a bad rufi last night.

Part 5

The Naturally Occurring: Mommie Nature Dearest

Killer Bees!

The Grim Rating:
A solid 9!
"Ya ever taken a gander at the CEO of QualiGrow? Even S'tan doesn't look that evil!"

How It'll Go Down: In light of the continued decline of the "good" bee population, QualiGrow, a multinational agricultural corporation, will develop what it hopes to be a more resilient good bee. This will involve attempting to rehabilitate Africanized killer bees. Crikey, what a messed up idea that was! The bad bees become worse and way more killerish.

Unfortunately, none of the QG geneticists (not to be confused with *GQ*—trust us) discover their blunder until the bees have been released into the wild. Once unleashed, they'll make short work of everything in their flight plan, including homo sapiens. Over time, our planet will become one lovely, pollinated field overflowing with fauna of every color, sorely lacking in human or animal life.

Estimated Length of Disaster: About thirty years.

Percentage of Population Affected: Not everyone will be stung to death, but estimates run as high as 99.2%.

Here's the buzz:

KILLER BEES BUCKET LIST

☐ Three words: Kevlar beekeeper suit.

☐ Buy multiple pet bears.

☐ It is believed that this particular breed of bee is calmed by the Motown classics, especially tunes featuring the sweetly tragic Tammi Terrell. We're with the bees on this one!

☐ Keep your safe room smoky.

☐ Go long on Calamine futures.

☐ Begin breeding your own brand of customized cowardly bees. Once freed, they'll lead the killer bees on a merry chase away from *your* location.

☐ If you're a female, step away from the swarm. There's a reason why they say, "Once you go yellow and black..."

☐ Assemble Navy Seal-type team to seek out the queen bee. Night vision goggles are a must and look terrific on you.

Deranged Birds!

The Grim Rating:

A dopey 5.1.

"Again, too many variables. But here's something you might enjoy—Hitchcock and I play Canasta every Sunday night. True story. It's a mutual admiration society—we enjoy each other's work."

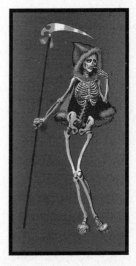

How It'll Go Down: The long-feared avian flu surfaces with a vengeance. And then it mutates. As a result, birds don't die but are, instead, feverish and testy. What was once that noisy flock of grackles in your backyard maple tree becomes a gaggle of grumpy grackles who want to gnaw on your neck and crap on your corpse. And the same goes for every type of bird, even the usually perky, caged parakeets who now, as a result of the malady, routinely try to kill their reflections in those cute swinging mirrors. Who's a pretty psycho bird?

For a culture that got so enamored with a game called Angry Birds, the irony will not be lost on us.

Estimated Length of Disaster: This is another one of those plot lines that's not written in stone (or suet). How the story turns out depends on the degree to which the military and cat population find a way to work together to ground the winged hellions.

Percentage of Population Affected: 42–82%, with an error rate of +/-40%. (Our math skills could use some work.)

Here's your peckish list:

SICK BIRDS BUCKET LIST

☐ Do *everything* possible not to resemble Tippi Hedren.

☐ Researchers tell us that by mixing baby aspirin into your birdfeeder blend, you can bring down their fevers and lessen the threat.

☐ Pull that sonic rifle you'd been working on out of the closet and finish it. For this disaster, adjust the output to "Death Metal." Warning: Do *not* aim at humans—could cause ear bleeds, bad dancing, and mosh pits.

☐ You'll know it's time to find a different home for your long-loved macaw when it starts staring at you and muttering, "Polly wants an Uzi."

☐ Screw the city ordinances—it's time for feline hoarding.

☐ When running for your life out in the open, move in a zigzag manner and stay as unpredictable as possible. The birds can't land on what they can't grab.

☐ Sunflower seeds and a shotgun. Get the picture?

☐ Despite what Mr. McCartney might think, his blackbird singing in the dead of night is more about "dead" than "night." So regardless of what soothing guitar chords you play, don't expect any compassion from *that* bird—he'll eat your eyes if given the chance.

☐ Interesting fact: the first wave of birds will be hummingbirds who will have learned the *Jaws* theme but, of course, in a much higher key.

Incredibly Bad Global Flatulence!

The Grim Rating:

Really? 0.8.

"How insulting—a fart catastrophe. This is *absolutely* beneath my notice. Don't get me wrong—I'll take the measly scraps, but I don't have to like 'em."

How It'll Go Down: No one knows how this one came about. Nevertheless, sulfur is natural and, thus, this is categorized as such.

This will be repulsive and stink even worse. Most every person on the planet will be suffering from the effects of continuous farting while simultaneously enduring the collective stench of everyone else's poots.

On the upside, the death toll won't be as severe as most other disasters. However, many humans would *prefer* to die rather than deal with the lingering farticulate matter. Several million won't survive due to the swirling sulfur haze. As Joni Mitchell wrote, "I really don't smell clouds at all."

Estimated Length of Disaster: About a month. This includes time allotted for the sulfur to disperse and the gagging to stop.

Percentage of Population Affected: Everyone will be affected, but probably only 5% will pass, so to speak.

Here's a stinker of a list:

GLOBAL FLATULENCE BUCKET LIST

☐ Beano. By the crate. And oxygen delivery too.

☐ Don't treat this one lightly. You might think this sounds humorous, like an outtake from *Blazing Saddles*, but the noise and smell will become overwhelming. Once this happens, the sound of laughter will be drowned out by farting and choking as far as the ear can hear.

☐ This could be a chance to make a buck. Start a company that fart-proofs people's houses. Convince owners that it's much like winterizing but taken to an absurd level. Get snappy uniforms. Company name? Hmmmm—Windbreaker Sealing Services?

☐ Airtight underwear may seem like a solution, but those grundies have been known to explode over time. Allow your bottom half to breathe even if your top half can't.

☐ Members of The Cabal are hoping to be put into a state of suspended animation so that they can avoid this event altogether. Such an approach can lead to being awakened in the thirty-second century by a talking ape.

☐ When grocery looting, head to the antacid aisle first.

☐ Work on not breathing through your mouth. You're *so* not going to want to do that.

Earthquakes and Tsunamis!

The Grim Rating:

C'mon, man! 2.8.

"I expect a hell of a lot more out of this duo than a sniveling score like this! They're lagging *far* behind their counterparts. If they can't do their jobs adequately, I'm sure I can find more enthusiastic disasters who would *gladly* sub for them."

How It'll Go Down: Earthquakes and tsunamis—they're the Martin and Lewis, nay, the soup and sandwich of the disaster world. Almost inseparable since their primeval partnership began, they're still going strong all these years later. Sure, they each do solo acts now and then, but they always find their way back to each other for their most ambitious projects. And now, they're about to be inducted into the Disaster Hall of Fame. It just shows to go ya that nothing beats teamwork.

This two-headed titan will stage its biggest event ever when the infamous Pacific Ocean's Ring of Fire (named by the late Johnny Cash, we believe) suffers a critical structural failure. As this spreads around the Ring, the west coasts of both North and South America will disintegrate and disappear, which will put a dent in sunbathing. Additionally, much of Asia and Australia will have their eastern seaboards deleted from the planet. New Zealand will sink like a stone, which is a shame because we were looking forward to that ninth Hobbit movie, *Baggins vs. Baggins: A Hobbit Divorce Tale*, set to be released in May of 2023.

Estimated Length of Disaster: Once the initial tectonic shift occurs, the rest will follow. It'll take a number of weeks, but by the end of it all, the Earth's landmass will have shrunk by 44%, which is not chump change.

Percentage of Population Affected: 33%. And when that's combined with the reduction in landmass, we're going to see a dynamic economic opportunity for savvy landlords!

A soggy list that also has the shakes—must've been a rough weekend:

EARTHQUAKES AND TSUNAMIS BUCKET LIST

☐ Like many of these other catastrophes, sometimes moving is the only solution. That secluded inland cabin (think Unabomber) is looking better all the time.

☐ If you choose to remain in an ill-fated coastal zone, work on your swimming skills. Goal #1: Be able to tread water for a week. And get one of those nifty rescue whistles like that gal had in *Titanic*. Practice blowing the whistle like crazy while treading water—you'll feel better about your level of preparedness.

☐ If you believe tubing in a tsunami will be hilarious, you've watched too much *Jackass*.

☐ Once Japan no longer exists, someone will still need to supply inappropriate Hentai material to the world. That could be you! Start working on drawings of chesty wood nymphs and wide-eyed sailor girls. It might be distasteful, but the paychecks will be hard to argue with!

☐ The employment picture in America will sharply improve as many formerly out-sourced jobs return to this country. Companies like Apple will move manufac-turing centers to Kentucky and Tennessee. Siri will develop a drawl.

☐ When Chicago becomes the new Hollywood, don't rebuild that disturbing wax museum.

☐ Bolivia won't be so landlocked anymore. Make time for a vacation to check out the newly expanded Pacific Ocean. And while you're there, don't forget to visit Bauxite World, the edu-mining history park for young and old alike.

☐ Alaskans will no longer be able to see Russia. Sorry. (You know, that sentence could be simpler: "Alaskans will no longer be.")

Mothra!

The Grim Rating:

Me no love you long time—1.7.

"This is what happens when a storyline depends on fairies—you get micro-dividends. Still, I love an occasional trip to Asia. It gives me a chance to claim a few pervy businessmen!"

How It'll Go Down: Dang, Japan gets a lot of action.

By utilizing the Japanese equivalent of the Freedom of Information Act, it's discovered that the original classic sci-fi film *Mothra* was actually a documentary. The sequels were, indeed, regular marginal movies, but the first flick was real and Mothra played herself. Once this is discovered, the question becomes, "Whatever happened to Mothra?"

Weeks later, a savvy reporter from the *Tokyo Tribune* tracks her down on a nearby island where she's been living in seclusion with her fairy

friends. During this time, Mothra hadn't taken care of herself, gaining quite a bit of weight and developing a nasty booze habit. When the journalist convinces her to come back to civilization for a TV interview, Mothra agrees only if she can be paid in liquor and moist, rotting matter.

Unfortunately, when she arrives, the pressure of being in the limelight once more is too much for the matronly moth. Mothra breaks down, binge drinks, and drunkenly takes out skyscrapers in ways that only a giant moth can. (Of course, the weight gain hasn't helped her flying skills, which now more closely resemble "falling skills.") This leaves the fairies little to do except buzz around the raging insect, singing their insipid song, and trying to talk sense into her. Some fairies are useless.

Estimated Length of Disaster: If international forces can't get it together or the Tojo Corporation doesn't intercede, we could have a moth-based assault lasting the better part of a year.

Percentage of Population Affected: Probably only the major cities of Japan.

Here's the Mothra of all lists:

MOTHRA BUCKET LIST

☐ Indoors and outdoors, everyone in Japan is going to have to learn to live with less light, at least if they want to survive. Put dimmers on every circuit. Replace high-wattage light bulbs with extra-low wattage. And *don't* use candles—that whole "moth to a flame" thing is valid. Remember: the darker you can make your environment, the less likely it is that the damn she-moth will be attracted to your area.

☐ Arm the fairies to the teeth. Convince 'em we're on their side and that we love their recently added floor show. (When they sing "Sisters," we just about crap our collective pants!) If they won't listen to reason, ice 'em and put scab fairies in their place who'll work for minimum wage.

☐ Research the theoretical effects of hormonal imbalance in female moths and how one counters such a thing. Yams?

☐ Invoke the name of the snake spirit, Nzambi, and bring forth the Mega Boa who will surely do battle with the obese hammered wench. Hey, speaking of snakes, what's on sale at The Reptile Roundup?

☐ Consult with the Godzilla conspiracy theorists to see if those dweebs have anything to offer. Is it possible there might be a bona fide Godzilla out there too? Logic says that if Raymond Burr was real, then why not Godzilla?

☐ Locate a gargantuan male moth to be Mothra's suitor. Make sure he's firing blanks before you introduce them.

☐ Build a bug zapper the size of the Transamerica Pyramid and get a couple of F-16s to border collie the bitch into it!

Cockroaches!

The Grim Rating:

Okie dokie, roachie—8.7!

"Cockroaches have sure come a long way from when I first knew 'em. They've made remarkable strides, particularly in the personal growth category. They've now got the potential to be a perennial powerhouse.

How It'll Go Down: In one of the most disgusting moments in history (even worse than the *Lady Hoggers* premiere), billions of cockroaches of every shape and size will stream out of a multitude of locations—a crevice in Budapest, a closet in Columbia, a manhole in a Manhattan alley, and on and on. At first, humans will be wondering what kind of publicity stunt they're witnessing. ("Do insects have flash mobs?" they'll wonder.) But once folks figure out this is real, they'll understand the true extent of the icky.

These cockroach hordes will be bolder than ever, no longer content to dive for a crumb on the floor. They'll be going for anything and everything, including the contents of your fridge, other bugs, birds, mammals, and humans. They'll resemble a murmuring of tiny Tasmanian devils, twirling and swirling in paths of destruction. (Who knew disgusting could be so poetic?)

A noted etymologist will explain, at a special session of the U.N., that this is nature's way of cleaning house. He'll relay this frightening fact: The towering amount of trash we throw into landfills, lakes, and oceans is creating a proportionate bug population designed to counter the effects of such excessive waste. With the roach infestation, apparently, nature will have fired the starter's pistol—the cleanup has begun.

Estimated Length of Disaster: If someone (are you listening, MIB?) can't figure out a way to put the hurt on the bugs, they'll strip the planet clean within five and a half years.

Percentage of Population Affected: Possibly as high as 92%. Once again, the colder climates will have an advantage…until the roaches adapt, that is.

A buggy list:

COCKROACHES BUCKET LIST

☐ Keeping your place tidy is always important, but during this time, you might want to make your home a Felix Unger kind of clean. That means no crumbs anywhere, a thorough Cloroxing daily, and no food left on the counter for more than fifteen seconds.

☐ It could be time to bring back those scary DDT fogging trucks from the '50s. Sure, the stuff was toxic, but fogging was festive!

☐ Under the cover of darkness, apply a layer of manure to your neighbor's lawn. The roaches may go there and forget about your crib.

☐ Invention idea: Oversized clown shoes with steel-tipped toes. This will give us a chance to stomp on the bugs and get a little exercise in the process! See if Vince Offer is willing to plug these.

☐ Researchers tell us that the little creepies will no longer be operating exclusively in the dark. However, that doesn't mean they're going to be especially fond of *very* bright lights. It would be prudent to keep your house lit up like a scene from *THX 1138.*

☐ No doubt about it—this is *absolutely* a legit opportunity to buy more snakes. When the wife starts to give you grief about your potential purchases, here's your pitch: "Snakes eat bugs and we've got an impending bug problem. See how that works, *honey?*" You can worry about your possible snake problem later. Meanwhile, go get that pretty little king you've had your eye on! And maybe the albino corn too!

☐ He (or she) who possesses the Sacred Scarab of Astonia will allegedly be able to control the insects of the planet. If you can get your hands on the Scarab, that would be excellent. You could be a superhero who directs bugs to do his or her bidding, like a diversified Ant-Man. But then, the plan goes awry and the Scarab overtakes your mind, driving you mad. It proceeds to tap into your darkest thoughts and directs you to get revenge on those three bullies from junior high. You laugh maniacally as you track each one down and the roaches clean their bones. Bwahahahaa!!!... Uhhh, okay, maybe the Scarab isn't the best idea.

☐ Is there a roach CEO that can be reasoned with concerning this invasion? What are the roaches' long-term goals? Where do they see themselves in five years? Would they be willing to back off if the planet's daily garbage was given directly to them? Open a dialogue.

☐ Quit watching *Starship Troopers*—it's hysterical, but won't help a thing.

Snakes!

The Grim Rating:
Pitiful—1.6.
"They're snakes. *And?*"

How It'll Go Down: Because of the popularity of this book and the possibly irresponsible suggestions within, snake collecting will become the latest craze. People will be putting their snakes in little sweaters and hats and posing with them for Christmas portraits. This trendy pursuit will create a multitude of problems. Folks will realize eventually that they overcommitted on snake purchases and can't afford to feed all those spring-loaded mouths. As a result, millions of snakes will be abandoned and released into the wild. What's worse, this generation of snakes will have no fear of humans and will expect to be fed.

Snakes will be everywhere. To say that the world will be crawling with snakes would be accurate. It'll be so bad, Samuel L. Jackson will weep.

Estimated Length of Disaster: Hard to say, but the duration will be greatly shortened once we open that chain of mongoose stores.

Percentage of Population Affected: 12%. No big deal, right?

Fangs for the memories:

SNAKES BUCKET LIST

☐ Don't take any more calls from Billy Jim at The Reptile Roundup (even if he's got a three-for-one deal going on water snakes). If you absolutely have to talk to him, see if he has a buyback program.

☐ *Do* take calls from that knowledgeable salesman at Mongoose Mania.

☐ Again, don't ever try to sue us. We didn't twist your arm and there was a disclaimer in the lone footnote early on. Please try to be more constructive with your proposed solutions.

☐ Raccoons eat snakes. Just a thought.

☐ Remove the twenty-two terrariums from your living room. Take them outside and tip them over gently. Play "Born Free," release a kilo of mice, and let nature take its course.

☐ Move on to a different hobby. Scorpions are kinda cool.

☐ When you hear that Billy Jim was killed by

a water moccasin, despite the unpleasant feelings you may have toward him, bring his family a thoughtful ham.

☐ Maybe your snake collection can be re-gifted to friends who can better afford the sizeable cricket bills.

☐ Foxes eat snakes. And bears too. Did you ever score those bears?

☐ Issue pink slips to the kids in Jakarta who've been knitting the long, skinny sweaters.

Final Score/Final Thoughts from the Grim Reapress

The Grim Rating:

It's been real—8.1!

All in all, I thought we had a rather successful journey. Hopefully, you've now got a number of things to consider regarding your future. And me, I've got *so much* to look forward to.

What have we learned here, other than that Mothra was a colossal lush? Well, I believe we've rediscovered much about ourselves; at least, I know I have.

Let's start by taking a look at the final tally (total of scores in each category divided by number of disasters):

☐ Sacred = 5.814

☐ Cosmic = 6.028

☐ Invasions = 4.981

☐ Man-Made = 6.900

☐ Nature = 4.243

And the winner is *YOU*! That's right, the numbers don't lie—humanity is its own worst enemy. Not only did you win with the highest total, but you *also* had the most entries in your category! You really know how to do yourselves in. Thanks!

I must say, I'm a bit disappointed in the Sacred and Nature categories. I expect a midrange performance like that from the Invasions, but not from the other two. I would suggest Sacred and Nature go back to the proverbial drawing board and see what they can do to step up their games. And Cosmic, it was close, but keep on keepin' on—you're gonna get there!

As for what else we've learned, I'll tell you this: The time I spent with you gave me a boost—a much-needed shot in the place where my arm used to be. I feel like I'm invigorated, ready to take on the world again and get back to doing what I do best—claiming the souls of dying unfortunates. Let me at 'em/you.

I hope you feel similarly emboldened and enthused about taking the passionate actions required to survive *and* thrive.

Assuming you don't accidentally off yourselves first.

Thanks for letting me into your lives—now I know where you live.

Oh, better go—I hear an air raid siren.

All the best,
G. R.

David P. Murphy is the author of *Zombies for Zombies: Advice and Etiquette for the Living Dead*, *Zombies for Zombies: The Play and Werk Buk*, *Ace Your Zombie Exam! The Official Ph.Z. Study Guide*, and *Rapturella and Other Apocalyptic Tales*. David is also a songwriter and producer of four CDs, *Shining in a Temporary Sun*, Henry Perry's *Effortless*, Camille Metoyer Moten's *A Simpler Christmas*, and Beth Asbjörson's *Gratitude*. His next album, *My Fraudulent Memoirs*, will be released in the fall of 2012. After twenty-five years in Los Angeles, David now resides in his hometown of Omaha, Nebraska, with his mutant orange cat, Beany. He has recently completed his newest musical, *anotherwhere*. For more information about David, please see www.davidpmurphy.com and the YouTube channel www.youtube.com/Z4Zbook.